KU-480-069

ENGLISH DRAWING
FROM SAMUEL COOPER
TO GWEN JOHN

ENGLISH DRAWING

FROM SAMUEL COOPER
TO GWEN JOHN

148 REPRODUCTIONS

———

Introduced and chosen by
Geoffrey Grigson

London

THAMES AND HUDSON

B55- 16451.

HERTFORDSHIRE
COUNTY LIBRARY
741.942
4330008

ALL RIGHTS RESERVED

PRINTED IN GREAT BRITAIN BY JARROLD AND SONS LTD NORWICH 1955

LIST OF PLATES

ENGLISH DRAWING

ENGLISH DRAWING has been more varied, more vigorous and more accomplished than is commonly supposed, Gainsborough, Rowlandson and Charles Keene, as I hope this book will show, not having been the only artists to leave drawings with an axiomatic quality, a quality of self-evident truth.

Perhaps that quality will hardly stand by itself as a definition of good drawing; it may be only to say that good is good or true is true. Indeed in choosing these drawings, mostly from the great collections of the British Museum and the Victoria and Albert Museum, I have had in mind some remarks by an English poet. Gerard Manley Hopkins asked himself why so much nineteenth-century drawing looked so well at a glance, and then appeared empty, null and cold. His answer was remarkable. Like Baudelaire or Victor Hugo, Hopkins was a poet draughtsman; he could himself draw, as plates in this volume show, with a delightful and convincing apprehension, which allows us to respect his opinion, even though the views of the man of letters upon painting or all kinds of pictorial art may so often be pointless or eccentric. At a time when Burne-Jones enjoyed a select international reputation and when to criticize him was to be heretical, Hopkins looked into his pictures. He was revolted by what he called their bad, unmasterly drawing. "Masterly execution", he declared, is the quality an artist requires most of all.

This "masterly execution" was "the begetting one's thought on paper", it was conveying life into the work and displaying it there, Hopkins continued, *not merely giving a suggestion on paper of a life that had only been in the artist's mind.*

Having the "creative gift", the artist's duty, according to Hopkins, is to bring that gift to its "puberty", to its manhood of masterly execution, without which nothing survives for long.

I like his image, that if masterly execution does not convey the life into the drawing and display it there, "the product is one of those hen's eggs that are good to eat and look just like live ones, but never hatch". "I think", he added, "they are called wind eggs: I believe most eggs for breakfast *are* wind eggs, and none the worse for it"—as a breakfast food.

Hopkins is the right man to quote upon English drawing for another reason—for the peculiar strength of his own relationship to the world of selected objects. I notice that "inscape", that famous word and concept of the creative life of Hopkins, has crept into Mr Aldous Huxley's report of his experiments with mescalin. The drug gave him a hallowed vision of reality. A poor visualizer, with the aid of mescalin Mr Huxley was able to see the glory of the folds of cloth in his own trouser-leg, let alone the glory of a table and of flowers (automobiles, by contrast, appeared to him in a new degree ridiculous, and vulgar) and this revelation reminded him, I suppose, of Hopkins—for example, of Hopkins praising the inscape of drapery in paintings by Mantegna.

For Hopkins the word inscape signified all the distinctiveness of objects or configurations, all of their inwardness, their totality, apprehended by their outwardness. Needing no mescalin, this poet, this marvellous visualizer, experienced the absolute *is*-ness or being of objects. Objects appeared to him to have a glory which he defined as a dull unconscious glory; as a poet he could transform this dull glory to the bright glory of conscious and intended praise. Mr Huxley, with the help of mescalin, also decided that sheer *is*-ness, sheer being, has its own sacramentality. So has the good drawing. The wind eggs, the drawings which do not hatch, come either from the bad moments of the good artist, or from the normal activity of the bad artist, equipped with a correctness of drawing, if you like, but lacking that hallowed mescalin vision of the inscapes of this world.

I do not mean, and Hopkins did not mean, that good drawing is a matter simply of relationship between art and nature. Chirico at one time wrote of Courbet, interpreting the wonder of his "realism", so called, as anything but realistic or prosaic, and remarking that what the artist sees with his eyes open is important, but that what he sees with his eyes shut is even more important. These two beholdings interact, and form the personal beholding, the personal style of the draughtsman: he is not simply an eye signalling to a hand which delimits an object with lines.

Nature in the simpler sense of what is beheld with the open eye takes a priority, in fact, only to the draughtsman's destruction. Many English draughtsmen have realized this, although they belong to a country where Nature, through philosophers and poets, has enjoyed a very large N. If that most tender and strong *petit maître*, Gwen John, orders herself to "impose" her style upon her work, if Whistler says that painting is the poetry of sight, if Charles Keene declares "I never could do any work without a foundation"—and no more—"from nature"; if Samuel Palmer affirms that although creation as well as art and vision must be studied, he will never, God help him, "be a naturalist by profession"; if Fuseli feels distracted by the interference of nature, if Gainsborough tells Lord Hardwicke that "if his Lordship wishes to have anything tollerable of the name of G., the subject altogether, as well as figures etc., must be of his own Brain" and not "*real Views* from Nature", and if Alexander Cozens uses "accidental forms without lines, from which ideas are presented to the mind", then all of these draughtsmen, all of these artists, are emphasizing what each one of them knows to be *himself*, the guide of the hand, the director of the open eye; they are emphasizing that element of all that is seen with the closed eye.

See with the eye in too permanent a closure, and you have the misbegotten, abysmally weak draughtsmanship of that great man, William Blake; you have all those other draughtsmen who give a suggestion on paper, in that phrase by Hopkins, "of a life that had only been in the artist's mind". Contrariwise, if nature is both your starting point and your finishing point, the consequence may be such incohesive and altogether unsacramental facsimiles as we are given in the drawing and the painting of the Pre-Raphaelites.

Where then is English drawing strong, and where is it weak? Protest or no protest, we have to push aside the wind egg artists, such eclectic draughtsmen, for example, as Alfred Stevens or Lord Leighton. Admiration for drawing of such men cannot be excused as a case of *de gustibus*, can only be condemned as a case of no gusto at all, of an incurable misapprehension of the energy, activity and substance of drawing, indeed of the substance of art itself.

But if we repeat that good drawing has an axiomatic quality, of self-evident truth, if we say with Hopkins that it displays masterly execution, if we say that it conveys a hallowed vision of reality, that it appears to convey an essence of being, then we are naming the great qualities, and ones which do occur, and occur again, in English work, from Samuel Cooper to Thornhill and Vanderbank, from Ramsay, Stubbs and Fuseli to Gainsborough and Rowlandson, from Constable, Bonington and Samuel Palmer to Charles Keene and Gwen John.

Good drawing always involves concern for what is drawn; and concern, perhaps, for being, for man, and for deity. To draw well is to be deeply concerned. It is not only to have acquired a language of design, since the technique of drawing is also a technique of vision and feeling; it is a technique of receptivity. The language of drawing is one of devotion, expressive feeling, expressive concern.

In English drawing, as compared with that of the greater schools, I should agree that this technique of expression and concern is too intermittent; not because artists have lacked the gift, the supply of which is a concern of luck and genetics, but because drawing as handwriting and drawing as concern have had to struggle among us too much by themselves, with too little aid. We have been too much, in this art, upon the edges of tradition, too intermittently in the hottest fire of European art, that fire which heats the gift, refines and sensitizes the concern, and compels masterly execution.

The centres of fire and incandescence do not come into being the moment a government or a borough council establishes a college of art. Usually within a single complex—the cultural complex of Europe, for example, now enlarged to a complex of Europe and the Americas, Australia, New Zealand, and South Africa— there has been at one period only one centre of supreme heat, supreme educative power, together with a few suburbs, or sub-centres. So far as I can tell, those

English artists who have drawn with most sustained concern and execution, who have come nearest to that puberty of the creative gift demanded by Hopkins, are the ones disciplined by the supreme centres or affined to them for a while in some strong degree. There are exceptions, but that is broadly true. Samuel Cooper (like Hilliard before him) was in France, and he was also in the Low Countries; Ramsay, Wilson, Alexander Cozens, Stubbs and Fuseli were in Italy. In the time of John Vanderbank, English-born though of Belgian descent, there began that intimacy with French drawing which lasted to Rowlandson, recurred in Bonington, and then after a dismal interval was resumed far on in the nineteenth century with Whistler, Sickert, and Gwen John.

I suspect we owe more than is yet allowed in histories of art to the influx of the Huguenots after the Edict of Nantes had been revoked in 1685; to a strict and, in a way, impersonal training of the pen in connexion with Huguenot silk-weaving, clockmaking and the crafts of goldsmith and silversmith. Vanderbank, son of the chief arras-maker of the Great Wardrobe, established a London drawing academy in 1720 in conjunction with the French refugee artist, Louis Chéron. Hogarth had early contact with Huguenot engravers and goldsmiths, the young Gainsborough worked for a silversmith, and by association with Gravelot, who taught him for a while, and Grignion, the Anglo-French draughtsman of a Huguenot family of goldsmiths, was brought into the lineage of Watteau. Stothard was apprenticed to a Spitalfields silk draughtsman, Rowlandson was in Paris as a young man and was also the protégé of a Huguenot aunt married to an uncle who was a silk-weaver.

In spite of the great efflorescence of painting in the eighteenth century, in spite of the climax reached in the great landscape painters of the early nineteenth century, in the home-trained vision of Turner, Constable, and Palmer, London never developed that professional self-sufficiency as a school of drawing, a school of concern and execution, which we have observed in the Italian cities, in the cities of the Low Countries, and in Paris. It came near to it, perhaps; and matters might have been different, a little different, had it not been for the cleavage of the Napoleonic Wars and the moods of aesthetic autarchy and self-conceit which ensued and endured through so many decades of the nineteenth century. So in spite of the stature of Turner and Constable, in spite of the intermittent excellence of their drawings, how instructive it is to compare the confined range of visual interest or competent draughtsmanship which their drawings betray (strong in landscape, weak in everything else, including the figure), with the more embracing interest and the more general competence of Gainsborough or Stubbs or Rowlandson before them, or in their own time of Bonington, who had the luck, in his short life, of working in Paris, and with Delacroix.

We should mistrust, I think, the search for special qualities in drawing which can be labelled English, Dutch, French, Italian, Spanish or German. The qualities we find are universal ones individually accented. My search has been for drawings which are works of art, rather than documents (although chronological order and selection of artists and drawings imply a comment upon the history of English art). Blake, least of English draughtsmen, asked that men should strive for immortal moments, which we might describe as moments which have a perpetual vitality (remembering the cautionary myth of asking to be immortal while neglecting to ask for everlasting youth). The good drawing, for all the varieties of gift at the back of it, is the recorded thought or moment of such perpetual youth and vitality; and not taking a relativist view, I do not believe it a convenient fancy that such recorded moments do endure and do overcome the changes of notion and belief. In drawing we have the moments direct and unadulterate, in a Palaeolithic animal drawing, an Egyptian drawing of a cat holding a fish, a drawing by Rembrandt or Rubens, a drawing of silks or a turning heel by Gainsborough, of bed-hangings or a suit of armour by Bonington, or of an elderly pauper or an adolescent girl by Gwen John.

So I have looked for drawings—why else should we look for them at all?—which emit some electricity. I must admit to caring little for that scholarship which seems interested more in the provenance of a drawing than in the drawing itself. A larger volume might have included architectural drawings or drawings by architects and might have included more of those artists of foreign birth who settled or worked for a while in England. There is something a little odious—and ridiculous—in raising an English umbrella over the greater of such men; and though they may have their moments, a consideration of Lely and Kneller really belongs in a different volume. Fuseli, though, is not only too important to leave out, he belongs by his own choice and his own career to London; so, in the following century, does Whistler—or at least he belongs half and half to London and Paris. And if Sickert comes from abroad, he was brought to England as a child and was English by feeling and intent. The limits of my selection are somewhat arbitrary; but they coincide more or less with the beginning and end of a tradition; and I have included no living draughtsmen, and no one who belongs to the new internationalism.

If there are omissions which seem to defy convention, I must plead, right or wrong, the application of a standard which precludes the drawing as wind egg or relic or antiquarian object. When a thorough examination of English drawing is made, as it must be some day, it should lead to a revision of who is who in English art. Lesser artists may draw well, no doubt, without being able to sustain their illumination through the stages of a picture. But we should be firm, as we look at English art, that unmasterly drawing, drawing that never rises above the wind egg, defeats all claim to be a master.

THE PLATES

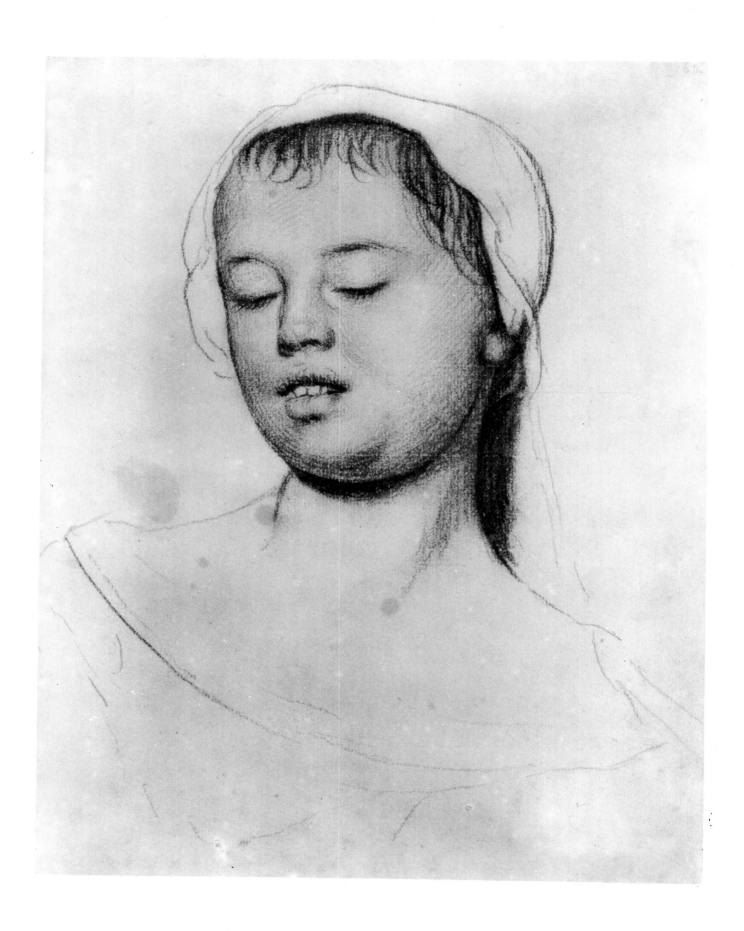

2

4

5

6

7

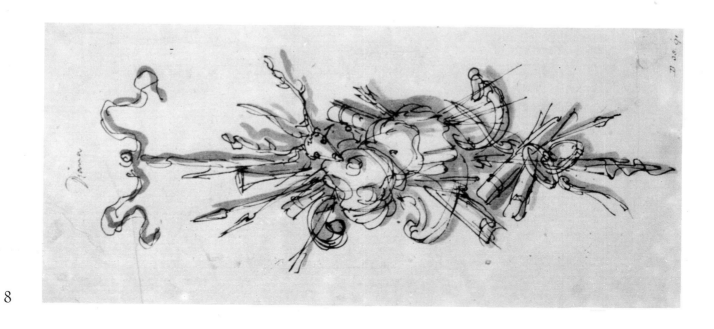

8

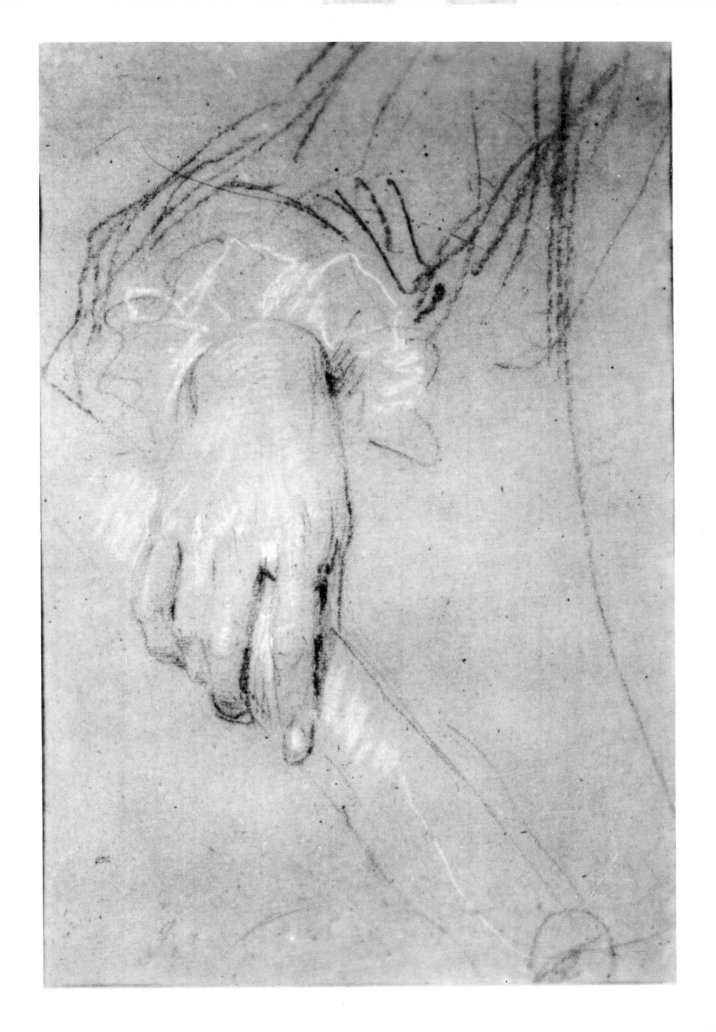

J·S·A·

12

13

14

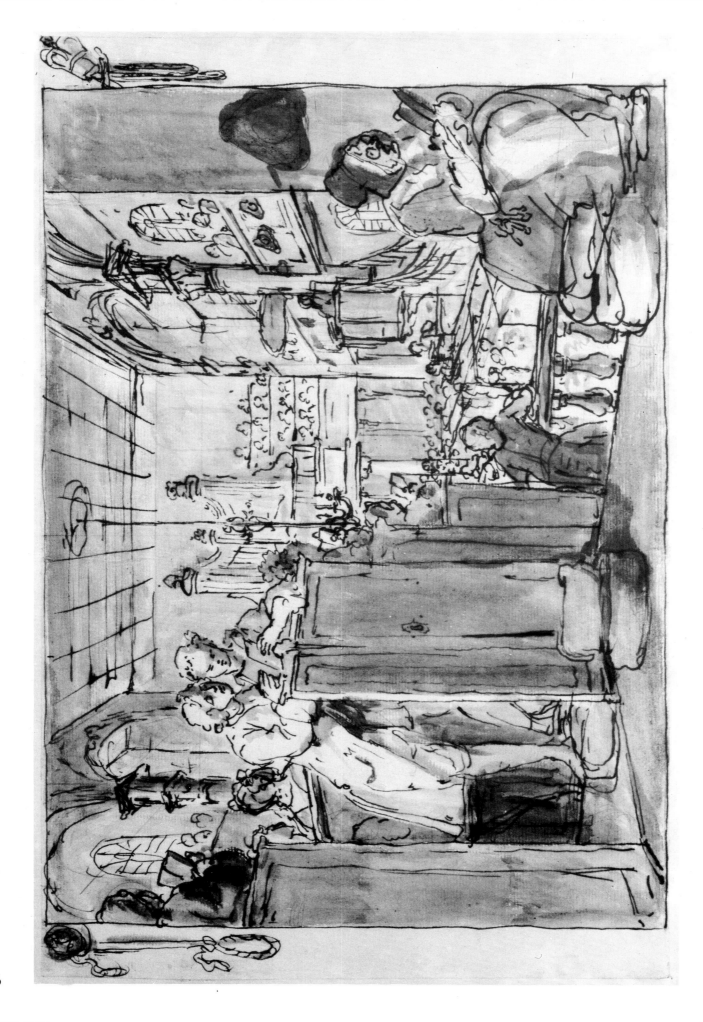

16

18

which so far surpass this European
† The grandeur of the eastern
depends as much on quantity as
on costliness. In a word it
richness

20

2054

23

24

27

31

32

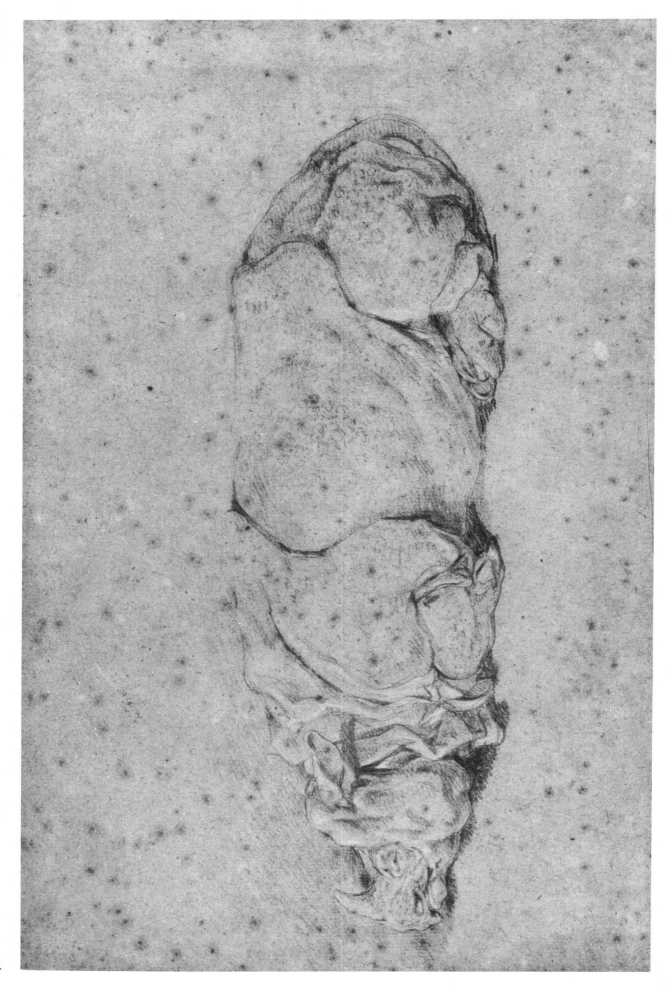

34

35

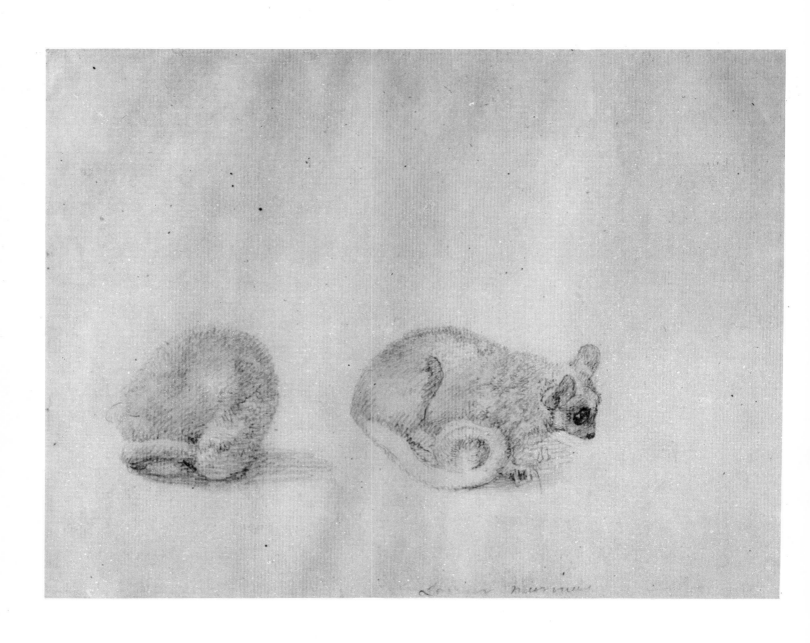

39

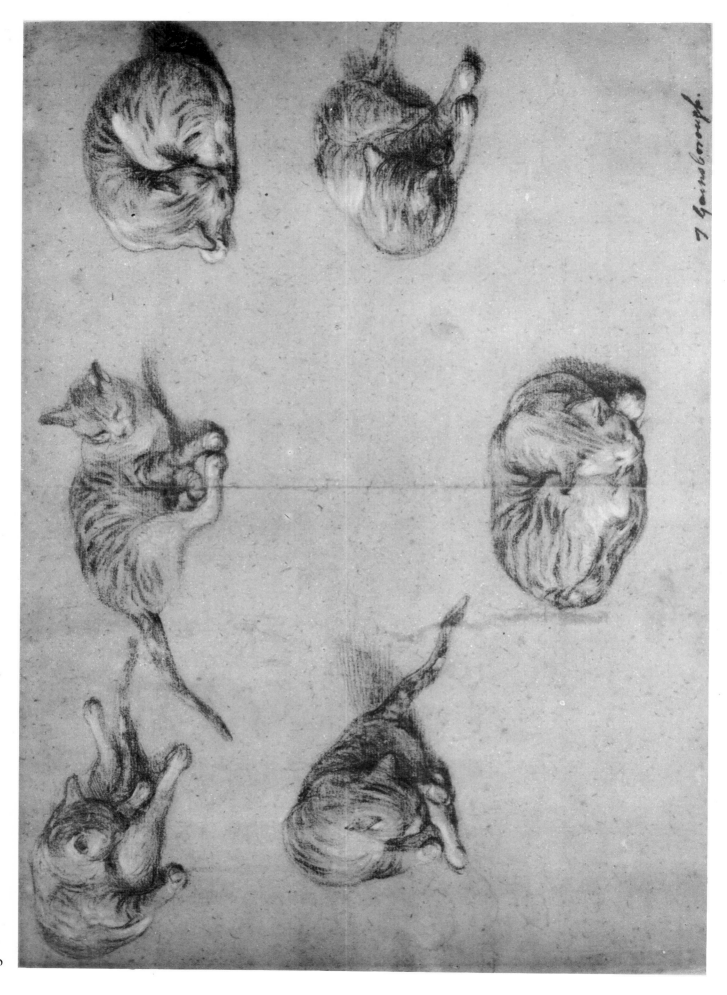

40

43

44

45

46

47

48

49

Sketch of the Galloping Horse

52

53

54

57

58

R. Jun. 15.

64

H. Füßli, Küste bei Margate

65

67

Joseph Farington 1787

68

LIZARD LIGHT HOUSE

69

Bailiffs outwitted.

The Drunken Husband

73

74

October 18 — 1813

78

6.

84

CCLX 101

94

Banks of the Canal, near
Newbury, Berks, June 4th 1821

96

97

F.D. Merwick
July 16 1835

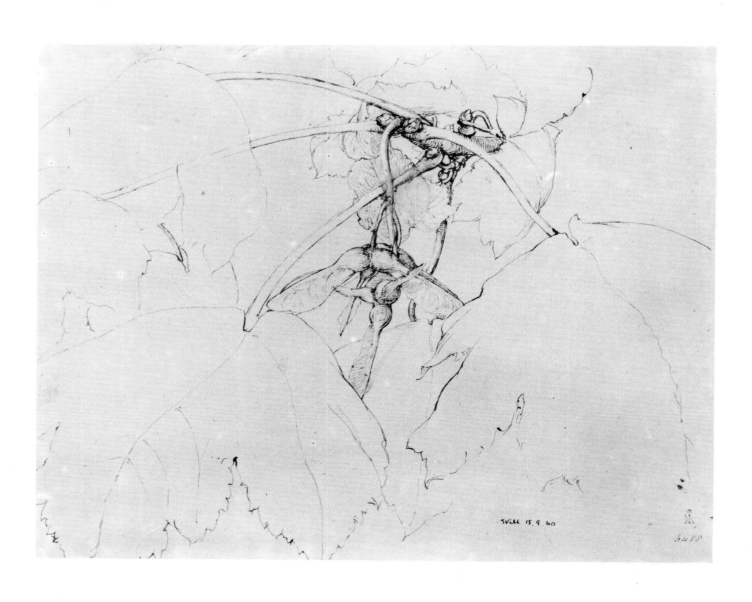

106

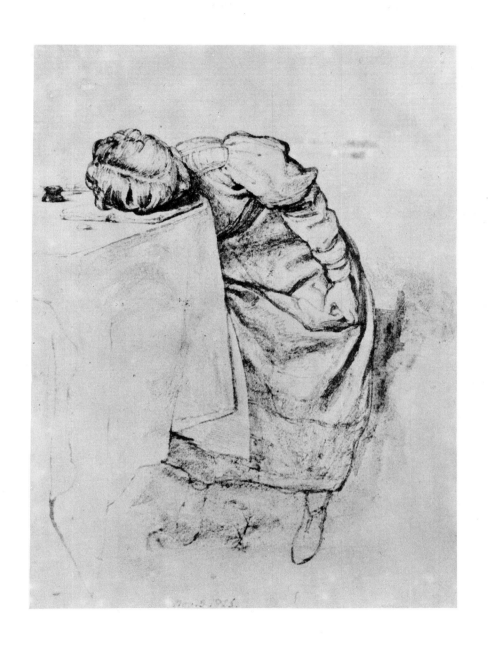

Gueaurrier
italien 1485

Brust
Rot

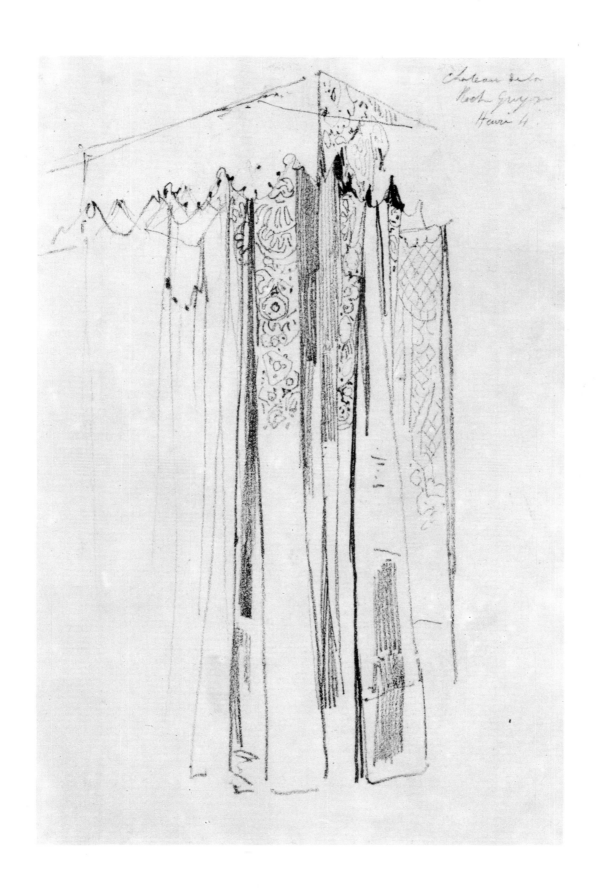

113

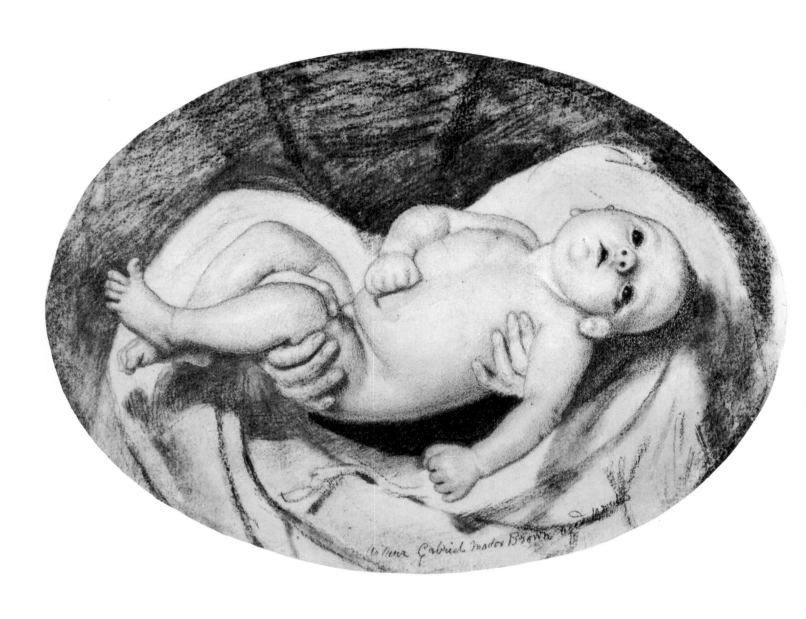

Accepted

John Everett Millais
1853

126

127

129

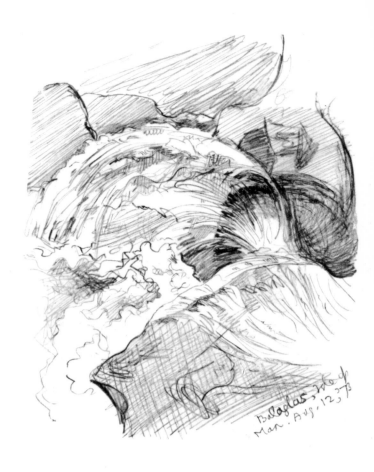

Ballaglas, Isle of
Man. Aug. 12, '73

Manor Farm, Shanklin.
July 8. 1866.

133

134

V. A. M.

Gwen John

Gwen John

140

Gwen John

142

BIOGRAPHICAL NOTES

BIOGRAPHICAL NOTES

SAMUEL COOPER
1609–1672

This *Angliae Apelles,* as he is called on his memorial in old St Pancras Church, in London, was the greatest of English miniature painters after Hilliard and one of the most delicately strong and talented of English artists during the seventeenth century. His father may have been John Cooper, music-master to Charles I, and lutanist. He was certainly taught by his uncle, the miniature painter John Hoskins, limner to Charles I, and he was influenced by van Dyck. After travelling and working abroad before the Civil War, in Holland as well as France, he settled to a practice in London which lasted into the Restoration. Thus he drew both Cromwell and Charles II. John Evelyn in his diary in 1662 describes holding the candle while Cooper was "crayoning of the King's face and head" for the new coinage, Cooper having chosen "the night and candle-light for the better finding out the shadows". One has a sight of him also in Pepys's diary, "the great limner in little", painting Mrs Pepys, talking French and exercising his skill in "playing and setting to the French lute". His friends included John Aubrey, Hobbes, Samuel Butler and possibly Milton. He was also appointed limner to Charles II.

See Basil Long, *British Miniaturists,* 1929; John Woodward, *Tudor and Stuart Drawings,* 1951; Ellis Waterhouse, *Painting in Britain, 1530–1790,* 1953.

CHARLES BEALE
1660–1714?

The second son of the artists Charles Beale and Mary Beale. In his childhood he copied van Dyck and Lely and was a pupil of the miniature painter Thomas Flatman. His chalk drawings at the British Museum were catalogued by Laurence Binyon as the work of his mother Mary Beale. More recently the researches of Mr H. S. Reitlinger and Mr Edward Croft-Murray, Keeper of Prints and Drawings at the British Museum, have established Charles Beale's identity as an artist. The Pierpont Morgan Library in New York owns a sketchbook which he began to use in 1679. In the Victoria and Albert Museum there is a portrait by him of the Earl of Lauderdale dated 1688, and in the Fitzwilliam Museum at Cambridge a portrait (possibly of the poet Dryden) signed and dated 1693. Nothing is known of Charles Beale after 1694. Mr Croft-Murray writes in the new (unpublished) catalogue of English drawings in the British Museum, that these intimate figure studies in red chalk of members and friends of his family "have apparently no counterpart in the native English art of the time, though they are paralleled by the characteristic studies of Dutch genre painters of the seventeenth century such as Gabriel Metsu, and Gerard van Honthurst".

See also *J. Pierpont Morgan Collection of Drawings by the Old Masters, formed by C. Fairfax Murray*, vol. III, 1912, and H. S. Reitlinger, "The Beale Drawings in the British Museum", *Burlington Magazine*, September 1922.

SIR JAMES THORNHILL
1675–1734

"History painter" during the short-lived flowering of English Baroque architecture. He was born into an impoverished family at Melcombe Regis, Dorset, and was helped in London by his great-uncle Thomas Sydenham, the physician, who placed him as an apprentice with Thomas Highmore and left him money towards his professional education.

Thornhill matured when new public buildings and the new mansions of public men called for decoration; and he made himself master enough of mythological, historical and allegorical schemes in Baroque space and movement to compete against Italian and French practitioners who came to London. No doubt he owed much to one of these, the French artist Louis Laguerre (1663–1721), who worked in Blenheim, Chatsworth and other houses. Friendship with Vanbrugh and Wren the architects, with men of science (he was a Fellow of the Royal Society), and with the writers Addison, Steele and Prior, indicated Thornhill's standing and his cast of mind. He designed the allegorical histories in Wren's Painted Hall at Greenwich Hospital (1708–27) and also painted the stories from the life of St Paul in the dome of St Paul's Cathedral (1716–19). He was appointed History Painter to the King in 1718, and Serjeant Painter to the King in 1720, the year also in which he was made Sir James, the first English-born artist to be honoured with a knighthood. The Baroque ebbed, and with it Thornhill's fame, so quickly and to such a degree that many of his decorative histories were expunged, and even now he is hardly accorded the place he deserves in English art. Thornhill's daughter married William Hogarth.

JOHN VANDERBANK
1694–1739

Portrait painter, son of John Vanderbank, chief arras-maker of the Great Wardrobe from 1689 to about 1727, whose atelier was in Great Queen Street, London. His father was

Belgian, but this young Vanderbank was born in London on 9th September, 1694. Portraits by him include *Sir Isaac Newton* (National Portrait Gallery, London, and Royal Society), *Thomas Guy* (Guy's Hospital), *Samuel Clarke* (National Portrait Gallery) and *Queen Caroline* (Duke of Richmond and Gordon).

With the Huguenot Louis Chéron, he established in 1720 a short-lived Academy of Painting in St Martin's Lane. He died of a wasting disease in 1739 and was buried in Marylebone Church. Vertue records that he had lived gallantly, spending on women and wine and marrying "a vain empty woman" who had been his mistress. "He might have carried all before him, but gave others room to exert, and blasted his reputation, yet still his superior merit in drawing, greatness of pencilling, spirit and composition, kept up to the last, in spite of the blemishes of his vanities." *Vertue Note Books*, III, *Walpole Society*, vol. XXII, 1934.

For details of his father, some of whose tapestries exist in the Victoria and Albert Museum and at Yale University, see W. G. Thomson, *A History of Tapestry*, 1930. See also Ellis Waterhouse, *Painting in Britain, 1530–1790*, 1953; and "Sir James Thornhill's Collection", in the *Burlington Magazine*, June 1943.

WILLIAM HOGARTH
1697–1764

Painter of moralities and portraits, born in London, the son of a schoolmaster from the North of England, who apprenticed him to an engraver of silver plate. He set up as an engraver on his own in 1720, studying also at the Chéron and Vanderbank academy in St Martin's Lane, and no doubt with Sir James Thornhill, with whose daughter he eloped in 1729.

He conceived that the painting and engraving of what he called "modern moral subjects" would bring him a livelihood. The six prints of his first series, *A Harlot's Progress*, appeared in 1732. With these and the eight scenes of *A Rake's Progress* (1735), the prints of *Marriage à la Mode* (1745) and of *Industry and Idleness* (1747), Hogarth made himself a champion of middle-class morality—something, in fact, of a pictorial counterpart to his friend Fielding the novelist and magistrate. He owed more than is commonly realized to the French art of the period, possibly to the respect for art and the practice of the arts among the Huguenot families of London. Hogarth had contact with the Huguenot engravers and goldsmiths of the Covent Garden neighbourhood.

Dr Antal has maintained that as a great artist Hogarth "was obliged to take up and summarise in himself, within his early development, the entire previous continental evolution". He practised, indeed, a Baroque art for those who lived above shop or warehouse. As a draughtsman Hogarth was not given to making studies after models or after nature—a discipline he consciously and deliberately rejected. He used pencil or pen rather to work out his compositions for painting or engraving and to discover the right action of his figures. In 1734 he established an academy in a court off St Martin's Lane, which succeeded and filled the vacuum left by the failure of Vanderbank's academy, enduring for more than thirty years.

See A. P. Oppé, *The Drawings of William Hogarth,* 1948; R. B. Beckett, *Hogarth,* 1949, and articles by F. Antal: "The Moral Purpose of Hogarth's Art", *Journal of the Warburg and Courtauld Institute,* vol. XV, 3–4, 1952; "Hogarth and his Borrowings", *Art Bulletin,* March 1947, and his review of Oppé's volume, *Art Bulletin,* December 1949.

JEAN BAPTISTE CLAUDE CHATELAIN
1710–1771

Painter, draughtsman and engraver. There is doubt whether he was born in France or England. However, early authorities treat him as English. Thus Basan, in his *Dictionnaire des Graveurs,* 1767, calls him "graveur Anglais moderne". Redgrave maintained that he was born in London in 1710 of Huguenot parents, though he had changed his name from Philippe to Chatelain. There were certainly both Philippes and Chatelains among the Huguenot families of London.

His forte was landscape, and engraving after the masters of landscape, including Rembrandt, Claude and Gaspar Poussin. The French-born engraver Vivarès worked with him and was his pupil. Chatelain and Vivarès were among the early interpreters of the scenery of the Lake District. According to Joseph Strutt's *Biographical Dictionary of Engravers,* 1785, Chatelain worked only when necessity compelled him—"with a piece of tobacco taken from his mouth, he would make an admirable drawing of a landscape". He died in poverty, after too heavy a meal, at the White Bear Inn, Piccadilly, Vivarès and other friends paying for his burial in the Poor Ground of the Poland Street workhouse (W. H. Manchée, "Huguenot London; Greater Soho" and "Huguenot London: City of Westminster: Soho", *Proceedings of the Huguenot Society of London,* vol. XVII, 1942–1946 and vol. XIV, 1929–1933). Chatelain's drawings have often been ascribed to Gainsborough.

See also *Fifty, Small, Original, and Elegant Views of the most Splendid Churches, Villages, Rural Prospects and Masterly Pieces of Architecture adjacent to London, Drawn by the eminent Mr Chatelain,* 1750, in which drawings by Chatelain are engraved (badly) by Henry Roberts.

ALLAN RAMSAY
1713–1784

Portrait painter, born at Edinburgh, son of Allan Ramsay, poet and wigmaker. He had some instruction at the short-lived Academy of St Luke in Edinburgh. In London he may have attended Chéron and Vanderbank's academy, and was certainly taught by the Swedish painter Hans Hysing. He went to Rome in 1736, where he attended the Académie Française, and was taught by Francesco Imperiale. In Naples he attended the studio of Francesco Solimena. His mature style owed much to the French influences of Quentin de la Tour, Perronneau and Nattier.

In part Ramsay's naturalness was a temperamental revulsion from the Baroque and the grand manner. Horace Walpole described his art as "all delicacy" in contrast to what he called the boldness and tempestuous colour of Reynolds, whose chief rival he was among the London portrait painters. Vertue admired his "true imitation of nature", praising in his portraits their "easy free likeness, their habits and dresses well disposed and airy", the tenderness of the flesh and the "shining, beautiful and clean" qualities of his silks and satins. Ramsay visited Italy again in 1754, 1775 and 1782. But before 1770 he had almost given up painting for literature. He corresponded with Diderot, Voltaire and Rousseau (though he rejected what he called "Rousseau's Nature—Nature on all Fours"). His friends included Hogarth and Carle Vanloo among artists; and among writers, Hume, Adam Smith, Samuel Johnson and Boswell.

See *Vertue Note Books*, III, *Walpole Society*, vol. XXII, 1934, and Alastair Smart's *Life and Art of Allan Ramsay*, 1952.

RICHARD WILSON
1713–1782

Landscape painter, born probably in 1713, at Penegoes, Montgomeryshire, where his father was the parson. In London he studied under the obscure portrait painter Thomas Wright, also attending the Hogarth academy in St Martin's Lane. His career began with portraiture, though he had painted landscape (influenced by George Lambert) before his journey to Italy in 1750. He was first in Venice, where he knew Zuccarelli, and where he was open to the work of Guardi and Marco Ricci. Moving to Rome, he sat for his portrait there to Mengs, in 1752. Claude now became dominant in his admiration; and Claude Joseph Vernet may have persuaded him to give up portraiture for landscape. The art of Gaspar Poussin and Cuyp also influenced him.

He returned to London about 1756, settled to landscape, and was a foundation member of the new Royal Academy in 1768. His landscape of skies filled with the tenderness and dimension of light, spreading over idealized, yet English scenes, was not greatly in demand; and he was not helped by his independence of character (exemplified in the story of Wilson and Sir Joshua Reynolds: Reynolds remarking that Gainsborough was the best landscape painter in England, Wilson replying: "You mean the best portrait painter"). These things reduced him to poverty: and poverty was accompanied with the bottle. He had some relief when the Royal Academy gave him the salaried office of librarian in 1776. Wilson left the capital for Wales in 1781, dying in Denbighshire the next year.

Ozias Humphrey recorded in 1773, "Mr Wilson says the best and most expeditious mode of drawing landskip from nature is with black chalk and a stump on brownish paper touched up with white", and Wilson told one of his pupils that chalk drawing of this kind was to be his sole discipline for a year—"to ground me in the principles of light and shade, without being dazzled and misled by the flutter of colours". As one would expect from this energizer of English landscape, Wilson's surviving drawings show a wide range of visual sympathy and concern.

See Brinsley Ford, *The Drawings of Richard Wilson*, 1951 (which includes too many of Wilson's weaker drawings), and W. G. Constable, *Richard Wilson*, 1953.

ALEXANDER COZENS
about 1717–1786

Landscape painter and an early master of water-colour, born in Russia, the son of an English shipbuilder employed by Peter the Great. In Russia he may have had some contact with Chinese landscape painting. The facts of his life are uncertain. In 1746 he was in Rome, where he knew Joseph Vernet. Settling in England, he was drawing-master, first at Christ's Hospital, then at Eton; and he was patronized by the young writer, connoisseur and millionaire, William Beckford, whose few comments on Cozens suggest a lonely, self-contained dreamer, with an eighteenth-century fondness for systematizing the unsystematic in relation to his art.

Of several books by Cozens the most famous is now the *New Method of Assisting the Invention in Drawing Original Compositions of Landscape* (1755 or 1756), in which he explains a system of making blots—making with ink, that is to say, "varied spots and shapes . . . producing accidental forms without lines, from which ideas are presented to the mind". The blot suggested a drawing, a more finished and meditated drawing: "The first operation in composing from the blot, is to make out the sketch, by giving meaning and coherence to the rude shapes, and aerial keeping to the casual light and dark masses of the blot." He quoted from Shakespeare:

> "This is an art
> Which does not mend Nature, change it rather; but
> The Art itself is Nature."

His vision of landscape unappreciated, Cozens died in London in 1786, and was buried at St James's, Piccadilly.

See A. P. Oppé, "A Roman sketch-book of Alexander Cozens", *Walpole Society*, vol. XVI, 1928, and A. P. Oppé, *Alexander and John Robert Cozens*, 1952.

GEORGE STUBBS
1724–1806

Painter of animals, portraits, conversation pieces and pastoral fancies. His father was a tanner in Liverpool, and Stubbs worked in the tannery till he was fifteen, developing a taste for anatomy. The painter Hamlet Winstanley gave him lessons. Before settling in London, he visited Rome in 1754, where he may have been in contact with Richard Wilson. His friend Ozias Humphrey wrote of this visit, "Let it not escape notice that Stubbs's motive for going thither was to convince himself that nature was and is always superior to art, whether Greek or Roman—and having received this conviction he immediately resolved upon returning home." Obviously as he shows the influence of Claude and Cuyp, for example, and of Potter, and a sense of classical order (derived from Poussin?), Stubbs's conviction that "nature is superior to art" emphasizes a chief characteristic of his own art—unremitting study of appearances. Fuseli accused his pictures of depending more "on the facsimilist's precision than the Painter's spirit", but this is the judgment of an artist concerned with the passions and energies of the History Painter. More sympathy for his aims and more careful exploration of his work reveal, in his paintings and their landscape setting, an earnest and convincing naturalism.

Stubbs was in London by 1758 or 1759, painting horse portraits and etching the plates for his *Anatomy of the Horse*, which did not appear till 1766. At the time of his death he was working with firmness and vigour on the fine plates of a second anatomical book, the *Comparative Anatomical Exposition of the Structure of the Human Body compared with that of a Tiger and a Common Fowl*, issued posthumously in 1817. Few of the many drawings and studies he is known to have made have yet come to light.

See Geoffrey Grigson, "George Stubbs, 1724–1806", *Signature*, No. 13, 1940; *George Stubbs, 1724–1806*, the catalogue of an exhibition, Walker Art Gallery, Liverpool, 1951; Ellis Waterhouse, *Painting in Britain, 1530–1790*, 1953; Basil Taylor, *Animal Painting in England*, 1955.

CHARLES GRIGNION
1717–1810

Engraver and draughtsman, born in London of a well-known Huguenot family of watch-makers, goldsmiths, etc., who were settled in the neighbourhood of Covent Garden (W. H. Manchée, "Huguenot London", *Proceedings of the Huguenot Society of London*, vol. XIII, 1923–9).

Grignion was one of those artists of Huguenot descent who linked the painting rooms of London with the elegance and draughtsmanship of the French School. As a boy he was sent over to Paris to work for a short while under the engraver J. P. Le Bas. Hubert François

Gravelot taught him to draw and engrave, according to Vertue, and he worked with the engraver Gerard Scotin. In London he drew at the academy in St Martin's Lane. At one time he was intimate with Gainsborough, no doubt when the young Gainsborough was employed by Gravelot. He also engraved for Hogarth and in 1755 he was a member of the committee which considered plans for a Royal Academy. Grignion outlived his time, dying at Kentish Town in the neglect and poverty of an extreme old age.

THOMAS GAINSBOROUGH
1727–1788

One of the most charming and effervescent masters of eighteenth-century Europe. He was one of the nine children of a cloth-merchant at Sudbury, in Suffolk. As a boy he was apprenticed to a London silversmith (cf. the early days of Hogarth), coming in contact with the French engraver, Hubert François Gravelot, who employed him and taught him to draw. Early acquaintance with Charles Grignion, who also worked and learned from Gravelot and worked in Paris under Le Bas, may have helped to direct his art. Other influences on him were van Dyck and no doubt Watteau, also Ruisdael and Wynants.

Leaving Ipswich for Bath in 1759, and Bath for London in 1774, he lived by portraiture rather than landscape, his practice and the practice of Reynolds emphasizing a temperamental division between the two artists and among their clients—a division between an inventive and personal portraiture and grand depiction, between society in elegance and humanity and society wearing its public face. In landscape Gainsborough's method was rather to invent than to paint directly from his constant delight in the world of appearances. Richard Wilson spoke of the "fried parsley" of his pictures, and indeed Gainsborough explained his attitude firmly in an undated letter to the Earl of Hardwicke: "With regard to *real Views* from Nature in this Country, he has never seen any Place that affords a subject equal to the poorest imitations of Gaspar or Claude.

"Paul Sanby is the only Man of Genius, he believes, who has employ'd his Pencil that way—Mr G. hopes that Lord Hardwicke will not mistake his meaning, but if his Lordship wishes to have anything tollerable of the name of G., the subject altogether, as well as figures, etc., must be of his own Brain. otherwise Lord Hardwicke will only pay for encouraging a Man out of his Way." (British Museum, Add. MSS. 35350.)

Gainsborough's drawings were frequently made as ends in themselves.

See W. T. Witley, *Thomas Gainsborough*, 1915; Lord Ronald Gower, *Gainsborough's Drawings*, 1906; Mary Woodhall, *Gainsborough's Landscape Drawings*, 1939; and Ellis Waterhouse, *Painting in Britain, 1530–1790*, 1953. Also Ellis Waterhouse, "Preliminary Check list of Portraits by Thomas Gainsborough", *Walpole Society*, vol. XXXIII, 1953.

SAWREY GILPIN
1733–1807

Born at Carlisle, the seventh of the sixteen children of an army captain with a taste for art, who belonged to a celebrated Cumberland family. His father articled him to Samuel Scott the marine painter in 1749. After leaving Scott in 1758, Gilpin made his name and livelihood as a painter of animals. His first patron was the elderly Duke of Cumberland. Gilpin rivalled George Stubbs, giving his animals and his compositions less of the monumental naturalism of Stubbs, but more energy in action and more restlessness, so that in a special degree his work also foreruns the romantic energies of James Ward, Carle Vernet, and Géricault. He followed Stubbs as President of the Incorporated Society of Artists in 1774, but for all his skill and all the "piety, gentleness and benevolence, added to an elegance and sweetness of manners that irresistably gained the admiration and esteem of all who knew him", it was not until 1797 that he was elected an R.A.

Gilpin's brother was William Gilpin "the tourist", amateur artist and theorist of the picturesque. See W. S. Sparrow, *British Sporting Artists*, 1922, and *A Book of Sporting Painters*, 1931; Basil Taylor, *Animal Painting in England*, 1955.

JOHN HAMILTON MORTIMER
1741–1779

Painter and draughtsman. Son of a miller at Eastbourne, and a pupil (together with his friend, Joseph Wright of Derby) of Thomas Hudson, of R. E. Pine and of Sir Joshua Reynolds, though he worked, it was said, to more purpose at the Duke of Richmond's school of antique casts in Privy Garden, Whitehall. He made an early reputation as a draughtsman, but since he died fairly young and since his favourite subjects were "the representations of Banditti, or of those transactions recorded in history, wherein the exertions of soldiers are principally employed, as also incantations, the frolics of monsters, and all those kind of scenes that personify 'Horrible imaginings' " (Edward Edwards, *Anecdotes of Painting*, 1808), his paintings disappeared quickly into a limbo from which few of them have yet emerged.

In style and subject Mortimer's finished drawings are indebted certainly to the etchings of Salvator Rosa and (like Goya's art) to the etched *capricci* of Tiepolo. He was also influenced by the dramatic monumentalism of Annibale Caracci. Designing from Shakespeare (e.g. Caliban), *Don Quixote*, etc., he has something in common with the spirit of *Sturm und Drang* and with his coevals, James Barry and Fuseli. Like them he was admired by William Blake. "While Sir Joshua was rolling in Riches", Blake recorded, "Barry was poor and unemploy'd except by his own energy; Mortimer was called a Madman, and only portrait painting applauded and rewarded by the Rich and Great. Reynolds and Gains-borough blotted and blurred one against the other and divided all the English world between them. Fuseli, indignant, almost hid himself. I am hid." Disapprobation of his subjects was extended to, and perhaps explains, the repeated stories of Mortimer's looseness and extravagant character. He was made an A.R.A. in 1778.

The best accounts of Mortimer are in Edwards, *op. cit.,* and Ellis Waterhouse, *Painting in Britain, 1530–1790.* See also Geoffrey Grigson, "Painters of the Abyss", *Architectural Review,* October 1950.

J. H. FUSELI
1741–1825

To give him his original name, Johann Heinrich Füssli was born into a distinguished German-Swiss family at Zürich. His father was a painter, and he himself took to painting and literature after a brief, uneasy time as a clergyman. He came to London in search of fame and freedom in 1764. Reynolds encouraged him. In 1770 he went to Rome for eight years' study of classical antiquity and Michelangelo. His drawings are also indebted to the works of Bacco Bandinelli (1488–1560). Fuseli returned to Zürich in 1778 and to London in 1779, where he lived till his death forty-six years later. He was elected R.A. in 1790 and made Keeper of the Academy in 1804.

English opinion has been unjust to the power of Fuseli because of the extravagances to which it drove him. As long ago as 1820 Hazlitt pronounced what is still the common sentence—that Fuseli's "vagaries and distortions" were German, and lay "like a nightmare on the breast of our native art". He was not a romantic. He stood firmly by classical principles and practice, having no care for the vague or infinite, aiming to seize the human moments of energy, terror, revenge, jealousy, passion, in a style of energetic pre-cision. "I do not wish to build a cottage," he said, "but to erect a pyramid", which, after all, is a regular precise building, neither Gothic nor picturesque nor romantic. Though his achievement was short of his aims, other artists were affected by his peculiarity, strength and independence. Blake and Ward he influenced directly. He was early in recognizing the force of Turner and Constable, and he stirred the spirit of Samuel Palmer.

Long ago it was said by Allan Cunningham that he lives most by his drawings: "Those who are only acquainted with Fuseli through his paintings know little of the extent of his genius; they should see him in his designs and drawings, to feel his power and know him rightly" (*Lives of the British Painters,* vol. II, 1830).

See Arnold Federmann, *Johann Heinrich Füssli,* 1927; Marcel Fischer, *Das Römische Skizzenbuch von Johann Heinrich Füssli,* 1942; Paul Ganz, *Die Zeichnungen Han Heinrich Füsslis,* 1947 (English edition, 1949); Nicholas Powell, *The Drawings of Henry Fuseli,* 1951. Also E. C. Mason, *The Mind of Henry Fuseli,* 1951.

JOSEPH FARINGTON
1747–1821

Landscape artist, born at Leigh, in Lancashire, the son of a Church of England clergyman. In 1763 he became a pupil of Richard Wilson, and he studied also at the Royal Academy schools. By his long life, his power as a senior Royal Academician and his devotion to Wilson's art, he linked the first genuine efflorescence of English landscape to the romanticism of Turner and Constable (thus in 1800 Constable was copying a Wilson of Hadrian's Villa which Farington lent him). His own art, panoramic, colder and more topographical, had at any rate a dignity of composition. Farington's charming and sedate coloured engravings make *The History of the Thames* (2 vols., folio, 1794–6) a notable book of its kind.

The publication of his diary — *The Farington Diary*, edited by James Greig, 1922–8 — has done much to illuminate the history of English painting in the first years of the nineteenth century.

THOMAS ROWLANDSON
1756–1827

The most fertile and inexhaustible of English draughtsmen. He was born in London, the son of a warehouseman, dealer and chapman near Spitalfields. His uncle, James Rowlandson, was a master silk-weaver, his aunt (Jane Chevalier before her marriage) coming from one of the Huguenot families of the London silk trade. Relations were close between Rowlandson and his widowed aunt, who left him the greater part of her small fortune (Bernard Falk, *Thomas Rowlandson: His Life and Art*, 1949). In other words, there is once more a link between an eighteenth-century English artist and the French colony in London, with its interest, either for silk-weaving or the crafts of goldsmith or silversmith, in drawing and design. Rowlandson's Huguenot connexion may explain his presence in Paris *c.* 1774, and his command of French; and Paris (where he is reputed to have had instruction in drawing) may partly explain his fluency and certainty of line. He studied also at the schools of the Royal Academy.

Rowlandson soon abandoned portraiture and history for genre, for his typical blend of landscape and comic observation, and for caricature. Eventually he took to book illustration. Hogarth and Mortimer may have contributed to his liking for caricature and the grotesque, Gainsborough unquestionably influenced him in his elegance and freedom of line, and he made a close study of the antique. But one must agree that French Rococo influence was paramount, mingled with a neo-classicism, which is not always remarked upon, though it links him to Stothard, Blake and others of his generation.

See A. P. Oppé, *Thomas Rowlandson: His Drawings and Water Colours*, 1923; Adrian Bury, *Rowlandson Drawings*, 1949; A. W. Heintzelman, *The Water Colour Drawings of Thomas Rowlandson*, New York, 1947.

JOHN ROBERT COZENS
1752–1797

Landscape painter in water-colours, son of the painter Alexander Cozens and nephew of the painter, R. E. Pine. He was born probably in London, and he was taught only, it appears, by his father.

Cozens was associated with the connoisseurs Payne Knight and Sir George Beaumont, the friend of Constable, Coleridge and Wordsworth; it was perhaps with Payne Knight that he visited Italy by way of Switzerland in 1776, staying there for three years. He visited Italy again in 1782, with his father's patron William Beckford. Few details have survived about his person or his life. He was a small man, dreamy, and a musician, with a liking for Handel. In 1793 his mind broke down, and he was placed in the care of Dr Monro, the artists' physician and patron, dying in December 1797. His finished water-colours, or "tinted drawings" are more personal, more an expression of mood, than his father's designs, or the landscape of Gainsborough or Farington. Fuseli, who detested what he called "the last branch of uninteresting subjects, that kind of landscape which is entirely occupied with the tame delineation of a given spot", declared that J. R. Cozens detected the arrangements of nature "with an enchanted eye", drawing them "with an enchanted hand". Cozens was an unquestionable influence on Turner and on Constable, who spoke of his work with reverential superlatives. Seven sketchbooks from his Italian journey of 1782–3 are preserved at Hamilton Palace (Duke of Hamilton).

See "Drawings and Sketches of John Robert Cozens", by C. F. Bell and Thomas Girtin, *Walpole Society*, vol. XXIII, 1935, and A. P. Oppé, *Alexander and John Robert Cozens*, 1952.

THOMAS STOTHARD
1755–1834

Illustrator and designer, painter of fantasies which were influenced by Titian, Rubens and Watteau, of landscape and of wall and ceiling decorations. Stothard was the son of the landlord of the Black Lion in Long Acre, in London, and was apprenticed first to a Spitalfields silk draughtsman. In 1777 he entered the Royal Academy schools. He received encouragement from Reynolds and Richard Wilson and lived to impart advice to Samuel Palmer. In 1794 he was made an R.A. and in 1812 became Librarian of the Royal Academy.

Stothard shared the neo-classic taste of his friends John Flaxman and William Blake (he quarrelled with Blake in 1806 over his commission to paint *The Pilgrimage to Canterbury*, now in the Tate Gallery). Though his once famous book illustrations are frequently insipid, too little notice is taken of Stothard's remarkable, unmannered landscape drawings in water-colour or water-colour and pen. These are markedly personal in colour and design, and no doubt influenced Samuel Palmer.

See A. E. Bray, *Life of Thomas Stothard*, 1851.

WILLIAM BLAKE
1757–1827

Painter, engraver and one of the major English poets. "Inspiration and Vision", said Blake, looking back over his life, "was then, and now is, and I hope always will remain, my Element, My Eternal Dwelling Place." Ascending to that element, Blake never allowed himself the discipline which makes a draughtsman; so despite its exultation, its frequent happiness of design, its tender flaming of colour and its force of ideas, there is in his pictorial work always a war between intention and a grotesque inadequacy of execution.

The son of a hosier, Blake was trained at a London drawing school and apprenticed to the engraver Basire, who for a while sent him to draw monuments, details, etc., at Westminster Abbey. He was also a student of the Academy schools, making his livelihood afterwards as a journeyman engraver whose poems, paintings and colour-printed books both intrigued and irritated his contemporaries. Many influences affected him—admirations for Raphael, Michelangelo and Dürer, for mediaeval sculpture and illumination, and for Mannerist qualities of excess, coupled with the soft neo-classicism of his age. Thus his friends were, on the one hand, Fuseli and Barry (to whom he wrote a poem which is now lost), and on the other, Stothard and Flaxman.

See Mona Wilson, *The Life of William Blake*, 1948; Laurence Binyon, *The Drawings and Engravings of William Blake*, 1922; Darrell Figgis, *The Paintings of William Blake*, 1925; Geoffrey Keynes, *The Pencil Drawings of William Blake*, 1929.

JOHN FLAXMAN
1755–1826

Sculptor, friend of Stothard and William Blake and the outstanding exponent of sentimental neo-classicism in England. He was born at York, son of the modeller John Flaxman, and was trained at the schools of the Royal Academy in London. After making designs for Wedgwood the potter, he studied in Rome from 1787 to 1794, becoming R.A. in 1800 and Professor of Sculpture at the Royal Academy in 1810. His work included statues, busts, and monuments which are scattered through the churches and cathedrals of England (India as well) and the engraved outline illustrations to the *Odyssey* (1793) and the *Iliad* (1795), which influenced Ingres and kept their fame and popularity into this century. Marble gives his designs an adventitious crispness and firmness which his drawings lack. Nevertheless, Flaxman's likings were wide enough to include Gothic and Indian sculpture and paintings by Uccello.

See W. G. Constable, *John Flaxman, 1755–1826*, 1927, and Sidney Colvin, *The Drawings of Flaxman at University College, London*, 1876.

THOMAS GIRTIN
1775–1802

Landscape painter in water-colours. Son of a brushmaker in Southwark, London, and pupil for a while of Edward Dayes and John Raphael Smith. With Turner, he worked at copying in the house of Dr Monro, the amateur and connoisseur who liked to "bring forward" young artists. He was influenced by the breadth and spirit of J. R. Cozens, and by the panoramic, light-filled, urban vision of Canaletto.

Girtin is rated too highly in accounts of English art; he is praised too much for what he might have been, or to put it another way, the unity, breadth and intensity of his latest work, which suggests an immanence in nature, has led to uncritical exclamations about the earlier more awkward, more ordinary topographical water-colours, which are like the work of his master, Edward Dayes. Nobility, though, is a fair word for a handful of the cosmic panoramic water-colours designed shortly before his death; especially for the water-colours he made in preparation for the Eidometropolis, his panorama of London which was on show in 1802, and for the better of his views of Paris, which were studies, no doubt for a second panorama.

See Laurence Binyon, *Thomas Girtin*, 1900; Randall Davies, *Thomas Girtin's Water-colours*, 1924; Martin Hardie, "A Sketchbook of Thomas Girtin", *Walpole Society*, vol. XXVII, 1939; T. Girtin and D. Loshak, *The Art of Thomas Girtin*, 1954.

WILLIAM DANIELL
1769–1837

Landscape painter and engraver of enormous output. Born at Chertsey, where his father was apparently (like his grandfather) landlord of the Swan Inn. As a boy he assisted, and was trained by, his uncle Thomas Daniell, who took him to India in 1785. Returning to London in 1794, he worked with his uncle on the famous aquatints of their *Oriental Scenery* (1795–1808). His own chief work was to design and engrave the 308 aquatints of *A Voyage around Great Britain*, in eight volumes, folio (1814–25). Daniell also painted landscapes in oil and water-colour, and was elected R.A. in 1822.

His work continues the tradition of Paul Sandby and Farington, adding to Farington's panoramic dignity an extra drama more in keeping with Daniell's own generation.

See Thomas Sutton, *The Daniells: Artists and Travellers*, 1955.

JOSEPH MALLORD WILLIAM TURNER
1775–1851

Turner's long painting life, enormous productivity of many kinds, and development from period to period as though he had been several artists in one, make him a difficult painter to apprehend. A theatrical, even melodramatic, side to him has prompted suspicions in those who forget that a personality upon such a scale is likely to involve inconsistencies and contradictions.

He was the son of a barber in Covent Garden, in London. For a while he studied under Thomas Malton (1748–1801), whose forte was the architectural view, entering the Royal Academy schools in 1789. He found his way more quickly than Constable, and was made A.R.A. in 1799 and R.A. in 1802. A series of oil sketches of cloud and river scenery painted c. 1807 show a lyrical earnestness, simplicity and intensity with which he is not always credited, and prove how far he had moved by this time from the older landscape, derived from Poussin and Claude (and Richard Wilson). Canaletto and Guardi helped his progress. By 1813 Turner (and those who were his followers without his force) were known as the White Painters, and caused dismay by their rejection of the old black and brown tonalities. By 1816 Hazlitt was reproving him for "the quackery of painting trees blue and yellow to produce the effect of green at a distance". His first visit to Italy in 1819 proved his power as well as his receptive creativity: he was strong enough to absorb and control southern light and colour without flinching or collapse in a series of his broadest, most richly unified and most unmannered water-colours.

The analysis of light and the quest for colour now absorbed him more and more and carried him equally far from this pitch of romantic naturalism and from his theatrical translation of history-painting into cosmic drama. Turner's water-colours at Petworth c. 1830–1—colour impressions on blue paper of interiors and landscapes—display the happiest and most ecstatic cleansing of colour vision; they are ejaculations of the purest feeling. In the paintings of his old age, Turner was independent of patrons, market and criticism. He had learned from Guardi to dissolve the line of the horizon and now sent his illuminated colour whirling in great triangles round a receding spiral. A good example is the *Snowstorm - Steamboat off a harbour's mouth* (Tate Gallery), exhibited in 1842. Violence or whirl of coloured light was counterpoised in this late period by light quivering in repose, as in *Norham Castle, Sunrise, c.* 1840–2 (Tate Gallery). Such painting Turner carried out in loneliness, caring little for good-humoured mockery and incomprehension.

His drawing, sometimes brilliant, sometimes cursory or slipshod, accords with a devouring impatience in his character and an impatience to come to his waves and whirling pulsations of colour.

See Sir Walter Armstrong, *Turner*, 1902; A. J. Finberg, *The Life of J. M. W. Turner, R.A.*, 1939; A. J. Finberg, *A complete Inventory of the Drawings of the Turner Bequest*, 1909; A. J. Finberg, *Turner's Sketches and Drawings*, 1910; A. J. Finberg, *Turner's Water-colours at Farnley Hall*, 1912; Thomas Ashby, *Turner's Visions of Rome*, 1925; A. J. Finberg, *In Venice with Turner*, 1930; Douglas Cooper (reproductions), *William Turner, 1775–1851*, 1949.

JOHN CONSTABLE
1776–1837

"Lui et Turner", wrote Delacroix, who had experienced the impact of the French discovery of Constable's paintings in 1824, *"sont des veritables réformateurs. Ils sont sorties de l'ornière des paysagistes anciens"*; which expresses the fact accurately.

Constable was born at East Bergholt, in Suffolk, to a well-to-do miller. Farington encouraged him when he came to London, and he entered the Academy schools in 1800. Claude, Ruisdael, Richard Wilson and Gainsborough were important to him, but he looked beneath the manners of earlier landscape for the elements which were essential and unaffected. Others who felt the need of a more direct relationship between nature and landscape were less honest and independent than Constable, allowing their newer feelings to be clamped inside older formulae of picture-making. Constable's certitude and his amalgam of pride and humility are summed up in a confession of his faith, his aim to achieve "a pure and unaffected representation of the scenes that may employ me". He also remarked that for himself painting was "another word for feeling", which indicates both his depth and his limitation.

Critical, and sarcastic over shams, but coming firmly to his own mind about his own practice (of a new picture for exhibition in 1820 Farington records that he "has not and does not intend to consult opinions upon it"), Constable had to wait a long while for a recognition, which was then tepid. He was elected A.R.A. in 1819, after being rejected several times, and was at last elected R.A. in 1829, five years after *The Haywain* and two other pictures by him had been exhibited in Paris and had won him a gold medal.

His tastes included a sober liking for geology—for the science of that landscape which he painted—and also, it seems, for the science of those cloud forms he sketched so thrillingly in oils.

See C. J. Holmes, *Constable and his Influence on Landscape Painting*, 1902; Lord Windsor, *John Constable, R.A.*, 1903; C. J. Holmes, *Constable, Gainsborough and Lucas*, 1921; A. Shirley, *The Published Mezzotints of David Lucas after John Constable, R.A.*, 1930; K. Clark, *The Haywain*, 1944; A. Shirley (reproductions), *John Constable, R.A.*, 1944, and *The Rainbow, A Portrait of John Constable*, 1949; Kurt Badt, *John Constable's Clouds*, 1950 (which links his cloud studies to early meteorological investigations, to the cloud interests of Goethe and the cloud painting of Blechen and Dahl); Peter Leslie, *Letters from John Constable, R.A., to C. R. Leslie, R.A.*, 1932; C. R. Leslie, *Memoirs of the Life of John Constable*, ed. A. Shirley, 1937.

JOHN SELL COTMAN
1782–1842

Painter and etcher, born at Norwich, the son of a hairdresser in poor circumstances. Cotman received no formal education in art schools. When he was sixteen he came to London, working for a while for Ackermann the fine art publisher, and then drawing and copying for Dr Monro, who had also employed Turner and Girtin.

Cotman was friendly with Turner, and was associated with Girtin in a drawing society. His own successful drawing was limited to the requirements of landscape, in which he broke from the eighteenth-century conventions into a water-colour style combining in shallow planes a naturalism, a deep-toned precision and a calmly ordered clairvoyance. It is best seen in his tree-filled landscapes of 1805 to 1810. Cotman's modern naturalism had little success. He retired from London to East Anglia as a drawing-master, continuing to paint, and teaching himself, under the influence of Piranesi, to make etchings of picturesque architecture.

See A. P. Oppé, *The Water Colour Drawings of John Sell Cotman*, 1923; C. F. Bell, *John Sell Cotman* (*The Bulwer Collection*), 1926; S. D. Kitson, *The Life of John Sell Cotman*, 1937.

WILLIAM MULREADY
1786–1863

Draughtsman, landscape and genre painter. Son of a leather breeches maker at Ennis, Co. Clare, Ireland, who migrated to London with his family. In London he became a student at the Academy schools in 1800. Banks the sculptor and John Varley gave him encouragement and instruction, though he denied having been any one's pupil (Farington, *Diary*, 16th October, 1815, unpublished entry). Mulready began with landscape, changing to genre early in his long career and rivalling Sir David Wilkie, whom he far surpassed in his drawings. He was conscious of the weakness of English drawing and deplored the way in which the Napoleonic Wars had prevented interchange between England and the severer discipline of Paris. Joseph Farington recorded in 1807 that Mulready was "reckoned to draw the best" at the Academy schools, though he "sets himself high upon it as if he had done his business".

In his genre pictures Mulready sold his talents to the market; they tend to be cold essays in a story-telling outside Mulready's real concern, which is more apparent in the honesty and effectiveness of his drawings. His work, though, is ill explored. Certainly his romantic realism foreruns the realism of English painting in the late 'forties and the 'fifties. Mulready became a Royal Academician in 1816.

See F. G. Stephens, *Memorials of William Mulready, R.A.*, 1890; Geoffrey Grigson, "The Drawings of William Mulready", *Image*, vol. 1, 1949.

JOHN LINNELL
1792–1882

Painter of landscape and portraits. Like Cotman, and his friends Mulready and G. R. Lewis and others, Linnell began as a romantic realist or romantic "naturalist"; he painted landscapes which were crisp and condensed. His early portraits, too, were direct to the last line and wrinkle, contradicting the social mask. As a student of the Academy schools Linnell was celebrated for his precocious drawing. Both John Varley and Mulready gave him instruction. He was the friend of Blake, and he was much affected by Michelangelo, Dürer, Lucas van Leyden, etc., and by religious primitivism, which he looked for in life as well as art. His work lost its articulation, repeating itself in a pastoralism altogether acceptable to Victorian collectors. Samuel Palmer, to his cost in some ways, though he owed him his introduction to Blake and the lesson he derived from Dürer, became Linnell's son-in-law.

See (though it is not to be trusted) *The Life of John Linnell,* by A. T. Story, 1892.

RICHARD PARKES BONINGTON
1802–1828

Painter of landscape and romantic history, son of Richard Bonington, county gaoler of Nottingham until 1797, and then portrait painter and topographical artist and art teacher and lace merchant in Calais and Paris. The family settled in Calais in 1817. There Bonington had instruction from the water-colourist, F. L. T. Francia (1773–1839), who had worked with Girtin. The Boningtons moved to Paris in 1819. By this time Delacroix and Bonington had met in the Louvre, where Bonington was making water-colour studies from Flemish landscape. He studied at the École des Beaux-Arts in 1819 and under Gros in 1820, visiting Flanders in 1823, London in 1825 (in company with Delacroix with whom he shared a studio for several weeks on his return to Paris), and Italy in 1826. Stricken with tuberculosis, he was taken back to London by his parents, dying there in 1828.

Many years after his death, Delacroix wrote that he had envied Bonington's "facile brush" and "coquettish touch". Here was a man "replete with feeling, whose skill nevertheless carried him away. It is this sacrifice of nobler qualities to an unlucky facility which has now lowered the reputation of his pictures, stamping them with the feebleness of a Vanloo" (*Journal,* 22nd November, 1853). See also his letter to Th. Thoré, 30th November, 1861, in which he says that Bonington "made diamonds which caress and flatter the eye, altogether apart from subject or verisimilitude". Bonington's French training developed his draughtsmanship to a degree which sets him apart from most of his English contemporaries. The British Museum owns two albums of drawings by Bonington. Reproductions from a third important album belonging to the Marquess of Lansdowne at Bowood will be found in Andrew Shirley's *Bonington,* 1940.

See also A. Dubuisson, *Bonington,* 1927; Atherton Curtis, *L'Œuvre lithographé et gravé de Richard Parkes Bonington,* 1939, and Sydney Race, *Notes on the Boningtons,* 1950.

SAMUEL PALMER
1805–1881

Visionary landscape painter, son of a London bookseller, whose marks were unworldliness and a taste for religious primitivism. He was the pupil of an obscure drawing-master, William Wate, and was much influenced by Flaxman, Stothard (a friend of the family), Linnell, Mulready, William Blake and Fuseli.

From Mulready he learned a "discipline of exactness", as he called it. Linnell (whose son-in-law he became) reinforced his mediaevalism by introducing him to engravings by Dürer and Lucas van Leyden. He also drew from the antique at the British Museum and was acquainted with Charles Ader's famous collection of early German and Flemish pictures. Friendship with Blake helped to keep him from a shallow romanticism, and from about 1827 to 1834 he lived mainly at Shoreham, in Kent, intensifying a pastoral and religious vision of landscape. In 1828 he wrote: "Mr Linnell tells me that by making studies of the Shoreham scenery I could get a thousand a year directly. Tho' I am making studies for Mr Linnell, I will, God help me, never be a naturalist by profession." Creation, he thought, must be studied, "as well as art and vision", since it sometimes poured "into the spiritual eye the radiance of Heaven": it was wonderful as "the veil of Heaven, through which her divine features are dimly smiling", as "the setting of the fable before the feast; the symphony before the tune; the prologue of the drama; a dream, and antepast, and proscenium of eternity".

After his marriage in 1838 and a visit to Italy, Palmer's mystical passion declined; and he was transformed into a competent yet not greatly distinguished water colourist, working by his experience of Venetian art.

See F. G. Stephens, *Notes on a Collection of Drawings, Paintings and Etchings by Samuel Palmer*, 1881; A. H. Palmer, *Samuel Palmer, A Memoir*, 1882; A. H. Palmer, *The Life and Letters of Samuel Palmer*, 1892; Geoffrey Grigson, *Samuel Palmer, The Visionary Years*, 1947.

CHARLES SAMUEL KEENE
1823–1891

Draughtsman, etcher and painter. Keene's father was a solicitor, but he chose drawing instead of the law and was apprenticed to the wood engraving firm of Whymper. Five years of apprenticeship contributed greatly no doubt to his meticulous, firm execution. He drew at the Clipstone Street Life Academy, and lived by working for *Punch* and also for *Once a Week*.

His essential loneliness in between the world of Rossetti and Burne-Jones and the world of academic idealism may be gauged by Leighton's condescending eulogy after his death, delivered at an Academy banquet—"Among the documents for the study of future days of middle-class and of humble English life, none will be more weighty than the vivid sketches of this great humourist." Edward Fitzgerald, the poet, made the nearer estimate when he wrote of Keene as "a man who can *reverence*, although a droll in *Punch*". His characteristic was not so much the humour in the *Punch* drawings (often of subjects thought up by his friends) as a selective and relentless truth, a strong and certain quality of design which earned him the admiration of Degas and Pissarro.

"Bad drawing somehow revolts me—much of it", he told Sickert; and he knew quite well that he was surrounded in his time by more than the usual quota of pretentiousness and incompetence, and that *Punch* was *Punch*, yet a livelihood. His business, however, was to draw and not criticize or condemn; he liked a motto used in his mother's family, *Je me contente.*

In drawing and etching Keene was affined to his friend, Whistler, other admirations including the work of Menzel with whom he corresponded, Chodowiecki, Holbein, Hogarth, Bewick and Stothard. He had a taste for early literature, he was a passionate player of bagpipes of every kind for the unphrased melancholy of their music, he studied early sixteenth-century herbals for their wood engravings, and collected flint implements. His tobacco he smoked in seventeenth-century pipes collected on the Thames foreshore. If he had months of leisure and liberty, his desire, he said, would be "to draw horses and riders from the life, to make bagpipe reeds, and to find a place where I could play the great pipes for six weeks without being heard and finally conquer them". A few *obiter dicta* on record are less simple than they appear—"Draw a thing as you see it", "If a man can draw, he can draw anything", "I never could do any work without a foundation from nature." With Whistler, he stands for a naked and strong reaction to English stylizations of the time.

See G. S. Layard, *Life and Letters of Charles Samuel Keene*, 2nd ed., 1892; Joseph Pennell, *The Work of Charles Keene*, 1897; M. H. Spielman, *Twenty-one Etchings by Charles Keene*, 1903; Sir Lionel Lindsay, *Charles Keene, The Artist's Artist*, 1934; F. L. Emanuel, *Charles Keene*, 1935; D. Hudson, *Charles Keene*, 1947; and *Drawings by Charles Keene, 1823–1891*, catalogue of an Arts Council exhibition with an Introduction by Kenneth Clark, 1952.

FORD MADOX BROWN
1821–1893

Painter of history, genre and landscape, born at Calais, the son of a retired naval purser. At Bruges he studied under A. J. F. Gregorius (1774–1853) and at Ghent under Pieter van Hanselaere (1786–1862), both of whom had been pupils of David. He was taught at a more important stage by Gustaaf Wappers (1803–74) at Antwerp. In 1840 he was in Paris copying at the Louvre, and possibly taking notice of Delacroix and Delaroche; in 1845 he met the German Nazarenes, Overbeck and Cornelius, in Rome. In England, where he associated with the Pre-Raphaelites, influencing them and being influenced by them, his painting moved from romantic history to the moral realism of such famous pictures as *Work* (1862–5) and *The Last of England* (1885). His landscapes of the same time have a more striking and stirring individuality.

Independence of mind, a raspy tongue (Ruskin, the critic and art dictator of London, he described as looking like "a cross between a demon and a tallow-chandler"), and radical leanings militated against his success; he was an uneven painter, dogged, but without the force, the freedom or the distinction of personality which might have raised him into an English Courbet. His art was damaged by his own difficulties of spirit.

See *The Exhibition of Work, and other Paintings by F. M. Brown*, 1865 (a catalogue with Brown's own explanations); F. M. Hueffer, *Ford Madox Brown: A Record of his Life and Work*, 1896; Robin Ironside and John Gere, *Pre-Raphaelite Painters*, 1948.

SIR JOHN EVERETT MILLAIS
1829–1896

Millais's talent never matured. "He remained a boy till the last", said Val Prinsep, not quite realizing that an adolescence of character was accompanied by an adolescent arrest— and then a decline—of his abilities. He was born at Southampton, the son of an amateur artist and musician from the Channel Islands. While still a child of ten, he entered the Academy schools (1840), soon doing all the things required of a prodigy. Flaxman and a neo-classic simplicity of outline may be marked as influences. In 1848 he and his friends joined in the Pre-Raphaelite Brotherhood, startling London by the tight, pointed naturalism of their early pictures.

Millais painted remarkably between 1849 and 1855 (*James Wyatt and his Granddaughter*, 1849; *Return of the Dove to the Ark*, 1851; *Order of Release*, 1853) under the drive of adolescence—all the more so when he depicted sex with sex. After his marriage to Ruskin's former wife in 1855, his art thinned out to a wide, ceaseless banality, his arrested nature now fitting him to become a public hero of the arts. He was made R.A. in 1863, a baronet in 1885, and at last President of the Royal Academy in 1896—which was the moment, according to Edward Lear, of the "Millais-nium of Art". Millais's loss of vision was on the whole so thorough that one has sympathy with the phrenologist who examined his head, not knowing that he had the famous painter before him, and told him he was a shrewd man of business, but utterly deficient in imagination, and incapable of being an artist.

See *Millais's Illustrations, A Collection of Drawings on Wood*, 1866; J. G. Millais, *The Life and Letters of Sir John Everett Millais*, 1899; Robin Ironside and John Gere, *Pre-Raphaelite Painters*, 1948.

CHARLES ALLSTON COLLINS
1828–1873

Painter, novelist and miscellaneous writer, son of the genre and landscape painter William Collins, brother of Wilkie Collins the novelist and son-in-law of Charles Dickens. Sir David Wilkie and his father encouraged him to become an artist. After a training at the Royal Academy schools, intimate friendship with Millais drew him to the moral realism of the Pre-Raphaelites. In 1850 Millais proposed that he should be a member of the Pre-Raphaelite Brotherhood, in place of James Collinson. Other brethren did not agree.

According to Redgrave's *Dictionary of Artists of the English School* (1878), Collins took up with art "rather as a duty than from choice"; he was an irresolute man, and it was perhaps irresolution and ill-health combined which turned him from painting. He painted few pictures after 1858, though he drew illustrations for his own *New Sentimental Journey* (1860), as well as the title page for his father-in-law's *Edwin Drood* (1870). His best pictures include the sharp, strongly individualized portrait of W. Bennet (1851), now in the Ashmolean Museum, Oxford. Collins was the model for Millais's painting of *The Huguenot* (1852).

JOHN ABBOT McNEILL WHISTLER
1834–1903

No outline of English drawing can do without some mention of Whistler, a renovator of English art after one of its slackest and most self-satisfied periods. He was born at Lowell, Mass., the son of an engineer who found work in Russia in 1843. Whistler as a boy studied for a while at the Imperial Academy of Fine Arts at St Petersburg. After a taste of London, he went back to America in 1849. For a while he worked as a draughtsman in the Coast Survey at Washington, then in 1855 left America for Paris and never returned.

His friend Fantin-Latour introduced him to the painting of Courbet, which was decisive in his career, teaching him a lesson which underlies the most evanescent of his later work—that naturalism needs to be translated into a pictorial self-sufficiency. Whistler gave himself the freedom of London and Paris, settling by the Thames, of which he made etchings in and after 1859. He was the rebel, the settler from outside never afraid either to continue to be himself or to upset the natives. By his etching and paintings, his writings and his libel action against Ruskin in 1878, he made the English realize again that painting was not, in the first place, anecdote or imitation; and that it was not fancy divorced altogether from energy or fact. Painting, Whistler emphasized, is "the poetry of sight", no less a harmony of colour than poetry is a harmony of sound. Though his work is too often equated only with his Nocturnes, the way in which it emphasized the right function of naturalism and the self-contained existence of the picture defeated both the Pre-Raphaelite art-as-the-addition-of-details and the new aestheticism. "Rossetti", he once said, "is not a painter, Rossetti is a ladies' maid." Whistler's English friends included Charles Keene; Sickert was his pupil.

See J. A. M. Whistler, *The Gentle Art of Making Enemies*, 1890, etc.: E. R. and J. Pennell, *The Life of J. M. Whistler*, 1908, and *The Whistler Journal*, 1921; T. Duret, *Histoire de J. Mc. N. Whistler*, 1904; O. H. Bacher, *With Whistler in Venice*, 1908; J. Laver, *Whistler*, 1930; E. G. Kennedy, *The Etched Work of Whistler*, 1910; C. Dodgson, *The Etchings of J. M. Whistler*, 1922.

FRANK HUDDLESTONE POTTER
1845–1887

Born in Bloomsbury, the youngest of the twelve children of a London solicitor and nephew of the musician Cipriani Potter (1792–1871). He was a student at Heatherley's School of Art and the Royal Academy schools, and also for a while at Antwerp. Delicacy of health, shyness and a severe stutter barred him from the world, and though he was not untouched by the prevailing sentimentality of English art in his rare paintings of children and girls, he worked with unusual independence, binding his canvases together with subtlety and firmness. He owed more to Whistler and the French—and to himself—than to Pre-Raphaelite, aesthetic or academic mannerisms.

His friends included John Yeats, the sage and painter, whose son, W. B. Yeats, gives recollections of Potter in his *Reveries over Childhood and Youth* (1915). Elizabeth Yeats remembered him painting with a dark glove on his right hand, so as not to be teased by the reflection of his hand in the varnish, Potter adding, "I will soon have to paint my face some dark colour." His early death was caused by enteritis. According to Yeats, "Potter had been very poor and had died from the effects of semi-starvation. He had lived so long on bread and tea that his stomach withered—I am sure that was the word used."

The Tate Gallery, London, owns seven paintings by Frank Potter, who is represented also at the Walker Art Gallery, Liverpool, and the Municipal Gallery, Dublin. See H. W. Wheeler's article in *The Studio*, vol. LXXII, 1918.

GERARD MANLEY HOPKINS
1844–1889

No full account of the drawings of this great poet has yet been written. He was the eldest child of Manley Hopkins, marine underwriter and Consul-General of the Hawaiian Islands in Great Britain. Two of his uncles were painters, as well as two of his brothers, Arthur

Hopkins (1847–1930) and Everard Hopkins (1860–1928). Hopkins drew as a boy at Highgate School, as an undergraduate at Balliol College, and intermittently throughout his life in the Society of Jesus, which he entered in 1868. He was influenced by Pre-Raphaelite realism, but was not content with the mere outside of things. In his drawings, no less than in his poems, he grasped at what he called the "inscape" of scenes or objects, their apprehensible, total, individuating essence.

Hopkins judged contemporary art often with acumen and truth. Discussing "the bad, the unmasterly drawing" of Burne-Jones, he denied him the "masterly execution" which conveys life into painting: "the life must be conveyed into the work and be displayed there, not suggested as having been in the artist's mind: otherwise the product is one of those hen's eggs that are good to eat and look just like live ones, but never hatch". In the artist Hopkins wanted (and too often missed) the "puberty", or coming to manhood, of the creative gift of masterly execution. He was not taken in by the weaknesses of a Leighton, a Millais, an Alma Tadema; whereas he remarked of a grisaille by Mantegna that his inscaping of drapery "is, I think, unequalled, it goes so deep". Hopkins's best drawings are informed and filled by existence itself.

See Humphry House, *Notebooks and Papers of Gerard Manley Hopkins*, 1937; C. C. Abbott, *The Correspondance of Gerard Manley Hopkins and Richard Watson Dixon*, 1935, Appendix III (a superficial judgment of the drawings), and John Pick, *Gerard Manley Hopkins, Priest and Poet*, 1942.

WALTER RICHARD SICKERT
1860–1942

"I am a pupil of Whistler, that is to say, at one remove of Courbet, and at two of Corot", wrote Sickert, though it does not altogether define his keepings. He was born at Munich, the eldest son of a German-Danish artist and an English mother, who brought their family to England in 1868. After education at King's College, London, he became an actor, abandoning the stage in 1881, and entering the Slade School of Art. Whistler became his master, and in Paris in 1883 he introduced himself to Degas, his friend until Degas's death. Whistler, Degas and Charles Keene were lifelong admirations; and he came to be influenced by Pissarro, by Cézanne, and by Vuillard and Bonnard.

Nevertheless, there is also a German element in his work, an element of Expressionism without its bite, balancing in him the element of Impressionism without its tenderness. So far as Sickert has his origins in Impressionism, he is less an artist making a new departure than an heir inheriting a capital accumulated between Courbet and Bonnard. He is the artist at the tail of a tradition; which gives his accomplished paintings and drawings a certain ghost quality or quality of reflection. Drawing he once defined as "the extraction from nature by eye and hand, of the limiting lines of an object", a cold definition answering to a certain coldness or disinterest frequent in his own drawing. Over all, Sickert's work appears that of an eclectic, competent, cosmopolitan, intelligent and widely inquisitive. His writings on art have wisdom, point, contrariness and a loftiness of wit.

See R. Emmons, *Life and Opinions of Walter Richard Sickert*, 1941; Lillian Browse, *Sickert*, 1943; W. R. Sickert, *A Free House*, 1947 (selected writings on art).

JOHN MACALLAN SWAN
1847–1910

Painter, sculptor and draughtsman. Born of Scottish parents at Old Brentford, studied in the art schools of Worcester, Lambeth and the Royal Academy, and in Paris, where Gérome in 1874 introduced him to Emmanuel Frémiet the sculptor of animals, and where he worked from Barye's *écorchés* at the École des Beaux-Arts. Like Barye, he drew animals at the Jardin des Plantes, and in later years he drew a great deal at the Zoological Gardens in London. Swan was made an R.A. in 1905. As a painter he gave way too much to academic idealism, which at times could also dissolve the grip and the energy of his drawings. These are to be found in many galleries in England and abroad.

See A. L. Baldry, *The Drawings of John Macallan, R.A.*, 1905; Sir Walter Armstrong's article in the *Dictionary of National Biography*, 2nd Supplement, vol. III, 1912; and *J. M. Swan*, by R. A. M. Stevenson, *Art Journal*, 1894.

GWENDOLEN MARY JOHN
1876–1939

Gwendolen Mary John was born at Haverfordwest, Pembrokeshire, the daughter of a solicitor. Edwin William John, and Augusta John. With her brother, the painter Augustus John, she was a student at the Slade School of Art in London. Moving to Paris, she studied under Whistler in his old age, and made friends with Rodin and the poet Rainer Maria Rilke. At Meudon, outside Paris (where Rodin died in 1917), she lived in some degree of seclusion and poverty. "*Vous avez de grandes facultés de sentir et de penser*," Rodin had declared to her. She painted the nuns, the orphans, and the ancient almswomen of Meudon. Proud and humble, gay and melancholy, a Catholic convert and a painter of masterly determination who cared to sell few of her pictures, she wrote of herself, "*Mon cœur est comme une mer qui a des petites vagues tristes, mais toutes les neuvièmes vagues sont grandes et heureuses.*"

Her brother has recorded other sayings and comments of Gwen John. "Do not be vague or wavering. Impose your style. Let it be simple and strong; the short strong stalks of flowers." Though she admired Rouault, she attended little to artists of her time. Thus when asked her opinion of an exhibition of Cézanne's water-colours, her reply, scarcely audible, was: "These are very good, but I much prefer my own." She collapsed at Dieppe, after a train journey to the sea, and died there in hospital on 13th September, 1939.

Gwen John's pictures became publicly known in 1946 when a Memorial exhibition was held at Matthiesen's gallery in London, followed soon after by a second exhibition organized by the Arts Council of Great Britain.

See the article by Augustus John, *Burlington Magazine*, October 1942, enlarged as a preface to the catalogue of the Memorial exhibition, reprinted in the catalogue of the Arts Council exhibition, and again, with omissions and additions, in Augustus John's *Chiaroscuro*, 1952.

NOTES ON THE PLATES

SAMUEL COOPER
1609–72

1

Thomas Alcock. Black chalk. $6\frac{7}{8} \times 4\frac{1}{4}$ ($17 \cdot 6 \times 10 \cdot 8$). Ashmolean Museum, Oxford.

A drawing which confirms the praise in his own century of Cooper's extraordinary talent "for a face and all dependencies of it, viz. the graceful and becoming air, the strength, relievo and noble spirit, the softness and tender liveliness of flesh and blood, and the loose and gentle management of the hair". Richard Graham in Dryden's translation of Du Fresnoy's Art of Painting, 1695 (quoted by Basil Long, British Miniaturists, 1929). The back-board of the frame was inscribed, "This picture was drawne for mee at the Earle of Westmorelands house at Apethorpe, in Northampton-Shire by the greate, (tho' little) limner, the then famous Mr. Cooper of Covent Garden: when I was eighteen years of age.

> Thomas Alcock
> preceptor".

CHARLES BEALE
1660–1714?

2

Head of a girl with her eyes shut. Red chalk, strengthened with black lead and black chalk. $8\frac{7}{8} \times 6\frac{3}{4}$ ($22 \cdot 6 \times 17 \cdot 2$). Pierpont Morgan Library, New York.

3

Young woman in a fur hat. Red chalk, strengthened with black lead and black chalk. $8\frac{7}{8} \times 6\frac{3}{4}$ ($22 \cdot 6 \times 17 \cdot 2$). Pierpont Morgan Library, New York.

4

Young man in a wig. Red chalk, strengthened with black lead and black chalk. $8\frac{7}{8} \times 6\frac{3}{4}$ ($22 \cdot 6 \times 17 \cdot 2$). Pierpont Morgan Library, New York.

SIR JAMES THORNHILL
1675–1734

5

Sketch for the decoration of a chimney-piece. Pen and brown ink and wash, over pencil. $11\frac{1}{4} \times 7\frac{1}{4}$ ($28 \cdot 4 \times 18 \cdot 4$). Inscribed in pencil in the artist's hand "4 ft. 3 3-1-$\frac{1}{4}$ is a common half-length this will admitt of being just that size." British Museum, 1865-6-10-1341.

Laurence Binyon (Catalogue of Drawings by British Artists) considered this was a drawing of a Speaker of the House of Commons in his chair, with members around.

6

Sketch for the corner of a ceiling. Pen and ink and brown wash, over pencil. $9\frac{1}{4} \times 14\frac{1}{2}$ ($23 \cdot 5 \times 36 \cdot 8$). Inscribed in the artist's hand "Chimney side". Victoria and Albert Museum, D 15–1891.

7

Sketch for a wall painting. Pen and brown ink and brown wash. $12\frac{1}{8} \times 10\frac{5}{8}$ ($30 \cdot 8 \times 27$). Inscribed on the back in pencil "Johnston". Victoria and Albert Museum, D 14–1891.

8

Attributes of Diana, Ceres and Apollo. Pen and brown ink and wash. $9\frac{1}{8} \times 4$ ($23 \times 10 \cdot 3$), $8\frac{3}{4} \times 3\frac{1}{2}$ ($22 \cdot 2 \times 8 \cdot 8$), $9\frac{1}{8} \times 3\frac{5}{8}$ ($23 \times 9 \cdot 3$). Inscribed, respectively, in the artist's hand "Diana", "Summer Ceres", "Apollo". Victoria and Albert Museum, D 38–1891, D 39–1891, D 40–1891.

9

Design for scenery of the opera Arsinoe, Queen of Cyprus, 1705. Pen, with brown and grey washes over red chalk. $7\frac{1}{8} \times 11\frac{5}{8}$ ($18 \times 29 \cdot 3$). Inscribed in the artist's hand "Arsinoe sleeping. Act, 1st. Scene 1st by moonlight". Victoria and Albert Museum, D 26–1891.

Arsinoe was performed at Drury Lane in 1705. The libretto was taken from the Italian, Thornhill matching the Italianism with scenic designs in the grand manner.

10

Sketch for a painted panel. Jupiter and other gods and goddesses above the falling Titans. Pen and brown ink and brown wash. Size of sheet 14½×6¼ (36·7×15·9). Victoria and Albert Museum, D 10–1891.

JOHN VANDERBANK
1694–1739

11

Study of a hand. Black chalk, heightened with white, on grey paper. 15¼×10 (39×25·5). Signed "Jn° V". Courtauld Institute, Witt Collection.

12

A young man. 1737. Pen and ink. 8¾×6½ (22·2×16·7). Signed and dated "Jn° V 1737". British Museum, 1856–8–15–75.

13

Horse and horseman. 1730. Pen and ink. 9¼×7½ (23·7×18·8). Signed and dated "Jn° V 1730". British Museum, 1856–8–15–83.

Apparently akin to the drawings which Vanderbank made, and which Josephus Sympson engraved (very badly) for Twenty-five Actions of the Manage Horse, *1729. According to the book, Vanderbank, "the better to execute his Ideas, was himself a Disciple in our Riding-Schools, and purchased a fine Horse as a Model for his Pencil". However, Sympson also states that the drawings were done "in his younger Years, before he arriv'd to his present Perfection".*

14

Satyrs and sleeping nymph. Pen and sepia wash, heightened with white, on brown paper. 7⅞×7 (19·8×17·8). British Museum, Fawkener 25–5213.

WILLIAM HOGARTH
1697–1764

15

Nude, half reclining. About 1740–5. Black chalk, heightened with white, on grey paper. 16¾×10½ (42·6×26·7). Pierpont Morgan Library, New York.

According to Edgar Wind, this is a study for Hogarth's lost painting of Danaë, though A. P. Oppé doubts the ascription to Hogarth (The Drawings of William Hogarth, *1948).*

16

The Industrious 'Prentice performing the duty of a Christian. About 1747. Pen, with brown ink and Indian ink wash, over pencil. 8⅜×12½ (21·3×32). British Museum, 1914–6–13–31.

A drawing for Plate 2 in the series of twelve engravings of Industry and Idleness *which Hogarth published in 1747.*

17

The Industrious 'Prentice grown rich and Sheriff of London. About 1747. Pen, with brown ink and Indian ink wash, over pencil. 8½×11½ (21·6×29·2). British Museum, 1896–7–10–18.

A drawing for Plate 8 in the series of twelve engravings of Industry and Idleness, *published in 1747.*

18

The Idle 'Prentice stealing from his mother. About 1747. Pen, with brown ink and Indian ink wash. 8⅜×11⅝ (21·3×29·5). British Museum, 1896–7–10–29.

A design for the series Industry and Idleness *which was not engraved.*

19

A Judge writing. Pen and ink, in the MS. of Hogarth's *Analysis of Beauty* (which was published in 1753), vol. I of second draft, folio 40, verso. Size of page 7⅞×6¼ (20×15·9). British Museum, Egerton MS. 3013.

J. B. C. CHATELAIN
1710–71

20

View on a river. Black chalk and pencil. 8¾×13⅜ (22·2×33·9). British Museum, 1872–10–12–3276.

21

Italian landscape. Pen and brown ink. 10¼×15⅜ (26×39). Signed "chatelain". British Museum, 1871–12–9–6316.

ALLAN RAMSAY
1713–84

22

Study of hand and book. Black chalk on blue paper. $9\frac{1}{8} \times 10\frac{5}{8}$ (23·2 × 27). National Gallery, Edinburgh, 2054.

23

Study of a hand holding a scroll. 1757. Black chalk on blue paper. $7\frac{1}{4} \times 7\frac{3}{8}$ (18·4 × 18·7). National Gallery, Edinburgh, 2114.

A study for the portrait of Galileo painted in 1757, now in the Master's Lodge, Trinity College, Cambridge. Ramsay devised the portrait for Robert Smith, Master of Trinity, who on his death in 1768 bequeathed it to the college. The head he took from the painting of Galileo by Justus Suttermans (1597–1681), which is now in the Uffizi.

24

Portrait of the artist. 1776. Red chalk. $11 \times 8\frac{1}{2}$ (28 × 21·6). Inscribed "drawn by himself in the Island of Ischia, August 1776". National Portrait Gallery, London, 1660.

RICHARD WILSON
1713–82

25

Thomas Jenkins. About 1753. Black chalk, heightened with white, on greenish-grey paper. $10\frac{3}{4} \times 7\frac{3}{4}$ (27·4 × 19·7). Pierpont Morgan Library, New York.

Thomas Jenkins was painter, banker, dealer in antiquities and cicerone in Rome. See Thomas Ashby, "Thomas Jenkins in Rome", Papers of the British School at Rome, vol. VI, 8, 1913.

26

A grotto. Black and white chalk on light brown paper. $6\frac{1}{2} \times 8\frac{3}{8}$ (16·6 × 21·3). British Museum, 1881-2-12-27.

27

Seated woman. Black chalk on grey paper. $10 \times 9\frac{1}{2}$ (25·5 × 24·1). Ashmolean Museum, Oxford.

28

Italian scene with column. Black chalk on grey paper. $10\frac{1}{4} \times 15\frac{7}{8}$ (26·1 × 40·4). Ashmolean Museum, Oxford.

29

Falls of Tivoli. Sepia over pencil, heightened with white, on pale brownish paper. $10\frac{5}{8} \times 16\frac{1}{4}$ (27 × 41·3). British Museum, 1873-12-13-129.

30

Study of foliage. Black chalk, heightened with white. $11\frac{3}{8} \times 17\frac{1}{8}$ (28·9 × 43·5). National Gallery, Edinburgh.

ALEXANDER COZENS
about 1717–86

31

Tree with distant mountain. Ink and brush. $8\frac{7}{8} \times 12$ (22·7 × 30·5). British Museum, 1941-12-13-717.

32

Mountain and tufty valley. Ink and brush. 9×12 (22·8 × 30·5). British Museum, 1941-12-13-715.

33

Hill and trees. Ink and brush. $5\frac{7}{8} \times 7\frac{1}{16}$ (15 × 18). British Museum, 198 a. 2 (page 6).

GEORGE STUBBS
1724–1806

34

Rhinoceros, 1772 (?). Black and white chalk on blue paper. $11\frac{1}{8} \times 17\frac{1}{4}$ (28·3 × 43·8). Basil Taylor, Esq.

Probably a drawing of the Indian rhinoceros exhibited at Pidcock's menagerie, in London, in 1772, of which Stubbs made the painting now in the Hunterian Collection, Royal College of Surgeons, and reproduced Taylor, Animal Painting in England, 1955, Plate I.

35

Lion lying down. Black and white chalk on blue paper. $11\frac{1}{8} \times 17\frac{1}{4}$ (28·3 × 43·8). Sir Bruce Ingram, London.

36

Studies of a lemur. 1773. Pencil. $7\frac{7}{8} \times 10\frac{1}{4}$ (19·8 × 26). Inscribed "Lemur murinus", and on back "from an animal alive in the possession of M. Tunstal, Esqre by Mr. Stubbs 3 papers of sketches Lemur murinus". British Museum, 1914–5–20–302.

The British Museum has another sheet of studies by Stubbs of the same creature.

37

A skinned horse. About 1776. Black chalk. $14\frac{1}{4} \times 7\frac{3}{4}$ (36·2 × 19·7). Royal Academy of Arts, London.

A finished drawing for the twelfth anatomical table of The Anatomy of the Horse. By George Stubbs, Painter, 1766.

CHARLES GRIGNION
1717–1810

38

Thomas Grignion, the artist's brother. 1737. Black chalk and stump, heightened with white, on blue paper. $13 \times 7\frac{1}{2}$ (33·2 × 18·9). Inscribed on back "Thos. Grignion of Great Russell Street Covent [Garden] Drawn by Charles Grignion Senr on Thomas's return from Paris Aged 24 years". British Museum, 1890–5–12–94.

THOMAS GAINSBOROUGH
1727–88

39

Study for the portrait of Mrs Thicknesse (Miss Anne Ford). 1760. Pencil, with slight brown and green watercolour washes. $13\frac{1}{4} \times 10\frac{1}{8}$ (33·8 × 25·8). British Museum, 1894–6–12–11.

Gainsborough's delightful portrait of Mrs Thicknesse (while she was still Miss Anne Ford) is now in the Cincinnati Art Museum. Like Gainsborough, Mrs Thicknesse was an amateur musician. The strange story of how Gainsborough acquired and returned her viol-da-gamba is told by his biographers.

40

Studies of a cat. Pencil on buff paper. $12\frac{1}{4} \times 17\frac{3}{8}$ (31·1 × 44·1). Signed lower right "T. Gainsborough". Rijksmuseum, Amsterdam.

41

The Music Party. Red chalk. $9\frac{1}{2} \times 12\frac{3}{4}$ (24·1 × 32·4). British Museum, 1889–7–24–371.

42

Woody landscape with figures and a fire. Black and white chalk and stump on blue paper. $12\frac{5}{8} \times 10\frac{7}{8}$ (32·1 × 27·6). Inscribed "Bought at Gainsborough Dupont's Sale, 1797". Victoria and Albert Museum, Dyce, 677.

43

Study of a lady. Black chalk and stump, heightened with white, on pale brown paper. $19\frac{1}{8} \times 12\frac{1}{4}$ (48·6 × 31·1). British Museum, 1897–4–10–20.

44

Study for the portrait of Miss Lloyd. About 1750–5. Black chalk. $7\frac{1}{2} \times 5\frac{7}{8}$ (18·9 × 15). Signed "T G". Pierpont Morgan Library, New York.

The early portrait of Miss Lloyd is now in the United States. The Pierpont Morgan Library contains another study for the composition.

45

Study of a lady. Black chalk and stump, heightened with white, on pale brown paper. $19\frac{1}{8} \times 12\frac{1}{4}$ (48·6 × 31·1). British Museum, 1897–4–10–20.

46

Study for the portrait of a young girl. Black and white chalk on grey paper. $17\frac{5}{8} \times 14$ (44·8 × 35·6). Pierpont Morgan Library, New York.

47

Study for portrait of a lady standing. Black and white chalk on toned paper. $16\frac{1}{8} \times 9$ (41 × 22·8). Pierpont Morgan Library, New York.

A note on the back of this drawing says that it was once owned by John Constable.

48

Landscape with trees and cattle. Black and white chalk on pale brown paper. $10 \times 12\frac{1}{2}$ (25·4×31·7). British Museum, 1910–2–12–251.

49

Woodcutter seated. About 1777–8. Charcoal and wash, heightened with white, on toned paper. $18\frac{3}{4} \times 11\frac{1}{2}$ (47·7×29). Leslie Wright Collection (now in the possession of his daughter Mrs Keith).

Related to Gainsborough's last picture, The Woodman and his Dog in a Storm, *now destroyed although an engraving and a smaller copy exist. The woodcutters in picture and drawing are clearly from the same model. (See illustrated souvenir of the Sassoon Exhibition of Gainsborough in aid of the Royal Northern Hospital, 1936.)*

50

Man with a child on horseback. Pen and brown and grey wash. $9\frac{3}{16} \times 14\frac{7}{16}$ (23·3×36·6). Ashmolean Museum, Oxford.

SAWREY GILPIN
1733–1807

51

The shepherd. Pencil. $9\frac{1}{2} \times 12\frac{5}{8}$ (24·1×31·9). Signed "S. Gi (lpin)". British Museum, 1868–3–28–626.

52

A road horse of the Duke of Cumberland. Pen and Indian ink over pencil. $9\frac{3}{8} \times 12\frac{1}{4}$ (23·7×31). Signed "S. Gilpin" and inscribed by the artist "One of the Duke's Road-horses". British Museum, 1868–3–8–628.

J. H. MORTIMER
1741–79

53

Reclining nude. Pen and wash. $8\frac{7}{8} \times 10\frac{7}{8}$ (22·7×27·6). Art Institute, Chicago.

Described by Ulrich Middeldorf, Burlington Magazine, December 1936.

54

Portrait of the artist. Pen and ink. 16×15 (40·7×38·2). British Museum, 1859–7–9–70.

55

Head of Niobe. Pen and ink. $7\frac{3}{4} \times 6\frac{1}{4}$ (19·7×16). Victoria and Albert Museum, D 707–1889.

56

Demon orchestra. Pen and ink. $6\frac{1}{8} \times 8\frac{1}{2}$ (15·6×21·6). British Museum, 198 c. 10 (No. 18).

From an album of drawings which belonged to the connoisseur Richard Payne Knight (1750–1824). A copy of this drawing by Rowlandson is also preserved in the British Museum.

57

Man fighting a sea monster. Pen and ink. $11\frac{3}{8} \times 8\frac{3}{8}$ (28·7×21·3). British Museum, 198 c. 10 (No. 9).

From the Payne Knight album (see above).

58

Winged monster bending over bones. Pen and ink. $5\frac{1}{8} \times 8\frac{1}{4}$ (13·1×20·9). British Museum, 198 c. 10 (No. 19).

From the Payne Knight album (see above).

59

Skaters. Pen and ink. $6\frac{1}{8} \times 4\frac{7}{8}$ (15·6×12·3). British Museum, 1861–4–13–14.

J. H. FUSELI
1741–1825

60

Odin receives foreknowledge of the death of Balder. About 1770–8. Pen and ink and wash. $11 \times 15\frac{7}{8}$ (27.9×40·4). British Museum, 198 b. 5.

From an album of drawings made in Rome between 1770 and 1778. The subject is from Thomas Gray's poem The Descent of Odin, *published in 1768 during Fuseli's first years in England. Odin, the King of Men, rides his coal-black horse "down the yawning steep" towards the abode of Hela, goddess of death, whom he invokes. She tells him Balder will be killed.*

Another version (Federmann, Plate 48) belongs to the National Museum, Stockholm.

61

Dante finds Ugolino in the ice of Cocytus. About 1774. Pen and ink and Indian ink wash. $17\frac{1}{2} \times 12\frac{5}{8}$ ($44\cdot4 \times 32\cdot1$). British Museum, 198 b. 5.

Also from the album of drawings made in Rome. The less powerful version in the Kunsthaus, Zürich, is dated August 1774.
Fuseli draws a moment in which terror and wonder are concentrated. With Virgil who guides him, Dante has been lowered by one of the giants of the ancient world (their huge feet are visible at the top of the drawing) into the bottom of all guilt, the bottom of all the universe, which is the everlastingly frozen marsh of Cocytus which receives the rivers of hell. Here Dante finds the traitors gripped in ice, among them Ugolino and Ruggieri. In Pisa, as leader of the Guelfs, Ugolino had conspired with Ruggieri the Ghibelline leader to betray his own grandson, and was then betrayed in turn by Ruggieri and left to die of starvation in his prison. In hunger he now bites at the nape of his betrayer, who is frozen with him into the ice, so that one head, says Dante, is like a cap to the other. He leaves his savage meal for a while to lift up his head and talk with Dante (Inferno, XXXII and XXXIII).

62

Woman before a mirror. About 1820. Black chalk and pencil, on paper with an 1820 water-mark. $12\frac{5}{8} \times 8$ ($32\cdot2 \times 20\cdot2$). Kunsthaus, Zürich, 1938–719.

63

Dante faints and falls before Paolo and Francesca. 1815. Crayon. $11\frac{3}{8} \times 7\frac{5}{8}$ ($28\cdot9 \times 19\cdot3$). Inscribed "K. Jun. 15".) Öffentliche Kunstsammlung, Basel.

Dante has fainted with pity after Francesca has explained to him the root of the earthly love between herself and Paolo, for which they are now tormented in hell (Inferno, V).

64

Two figures on a cliff. About 1790–2. Pen and ink. $9\frac{7}{8} \times 8$ ($25\cdot2 \times 20\cdot3$). Kunsthaus, Zürich.

Sketched probably on the Thames Estuary at some point north of the Dover Road, from which the Essex shore was still visible.

65

Two women and a man on the edge of the Thames Estuary. About 1790–2. Pen and ink. $9\frac{7}{8} \times 8$ ($25\cdot2 \times 20\cdot3$). On the back of the preceding drawing, *Two figures on a cliff.* Kunsthaus, Zürich.

66

Portrait of the artist. About 1773. Pencil. $10\frac{5}{8} \times 7\frac{5}{8}$ ($27 \times 19\cdot3$). Inscribed "Fuseli". Kunsthaus, Zürich, 1940–186 (page 104).

From an album of drawings made during Fuseli's Roman years, 1770–8. His friend Lavater wrote of Fuseli, "His look is lightning, his word a thunderstorm: his jest is death, his revenge hell. At close quarters he is not to be endured. He cannot breathe one common breath" (Lavater to Herder in 1773—Heinrich Füssli: Briefe, ed. Walter Muschg, 1942).

67

Lady Hamilton. About 1782–6. Pencil, heightened with white. $15\frac{3}{8} \times 11$ ($39 \times 27\cdot8$). Inscribed "Lady Hamilton by H. Fuseli, R.A." Kunsthaus, Zürich, 1938–724.

Lady Hamilton had the electricity and vivacity which Fuseli looked for in women. He made this likeness of her probably when she was kept by the Hon. Charles Greville between 1782 and 1786 (as Emily Hart). Romney during these years painted her several times in various guises, e.g. as a nun praying and as Sensibility, face to face with a sensitive plant. "In her youth", Cunningham says in his Lives of the British Painters, "she took her beauty freely to the market of art—exposing her charms without reserve." In 1786 Greville passed her on to his uncle, Sir William Hamilton, who married her in 1791. See J. T. H. Bailey, Emma Lady Hamilton, with a catalogue of her published portraits, 1905.

JOSEPH FARINGTON
1747–1821

68

Landscape with castle. 1787. Pen and brown ink and Indian ink wash, squared for transference. $11\frac{1}{2} \times 8\frac{3}{4}$ ($29\cdot2 \times 22\cdot2$). Signed and dated "Joseph Farington, 1787". Tate Gallery, 4297.

THOMAS ROWLANDSON
1756–1827

69

The Lizard lighthouse. Pen and ink and water-colour washes. $5\frac{5}{8} \times 7$ ($14\cdot2 \times 17\cdot7$). Inscribed "LIZARD LIGHT HOUSE". British Museum, L.B.45 (page 53).

70

A negro slave. Pen and brown ink and slight water-colour. $6\frac{5}{8} \times 5\frac{1}{8}$ (16·9 × 13·1). British Museum, L.B.45 (page 26).

71 (above)

In the Mall. Pen and Indian ink wash with slight water-colour tint. $3\frac{3}{8} \times 5\frac{1}{2}$ (8·6 × 14·2). British Museum, L.B.45 (page 1).

71 (below)

The bailiffs outwitted. Pen and Indian ink wash with slight water-colour tint. $4\frac{1}{4} \times 5\frac{3}{4}$ (10·9 × 14·7). British Museum, L.B.45 (page 20c).

72

The drunken husband. Pen and brown ink with Indian ink wash and slight water-colour tint. $7\frac{1}{4} \times 9\frac{1}{4}$ (18·3 × 23·6). Inscribed "The Drunken Husband". British Museum, 1943–11–13–115.

73

The prize fight. Pen and brown ink and Indian ink wash with slight blue and red water-colour. $7\frac{5}{8} \times 12\frac{1}{4}$ (19·2 × 31). British Museum, 1856–7–12–937.

74

The Cock Tavern. Pen and wash. $6\frac{1}{2} \times 9\frac{1}{4}$ (16·6 × 23·6). Inscribed "Rowlandson". Gilbert Davies, Esq., London.

J. R. COZENS
1752–97

75

Lake of Klönthal. Pen and thin washes of Indian ink and water-colour. $9\frac{1}{16} \times 13\frac{15}{16}$ (22·9 × 35·4). Inscribed on the back "Lake of Klonthalen from the East No 21". British Museum, 1900–4–11–28.

76

View on the Reichenbach. Pen and thin washes of Indian ink and water-colour. $14 \times 9\frac{1}{8}$ (35·6 × 23·2). Inscribed on the back "No. 14". British Museum, 1900–4–11–22.

THOMAS STOTHARD
1755–1834

77

The Avon at Clifton. 1813. Pen and ink and water-colour. $8 \times 10\frac{3}{8}$ (20·1 × 26·4). Dated in the artist's hand, "Oct 9 & 11, 1813". British Museum, 1884–2–9–25.

78

Intemperance: design for a staircase painting. 1802. Pen and ink with sepia and blue washes. $8\frac{3}{8} \times 9\frac{1}{4}$ (21·3 × 23·3). British Museum, 1889–6–3–264.

One of the designs for decorations at Burghley House, near Stamford, which Stothard carried out for the Marquis of Exeter, 1799–1803. The central figures are Antony and Cleopatra, who drops the pearl into the cup. An oil sketch for Intemperance *belongs to the Tate Gallery.*

WILLIAM BLAKE
1757–1827

79

Studies for America. About 1793. Pen and ink with light pink water-colour. $11\frac{5}{8} \times 6\frac{5}{8}$ (29·3 × 17). Inscribed bottom right "for America". British Museum, 1885–5–9–1617.

Blake colour-printed his America, a Prophecy *at Lambeth in 1793. It contains much of his firmest and strongest drawing, more related to the world of objects. In the book the dragon figure is changed from female to bearded male.*

> "Washington spoke: Friends of America look
> over the Atlantic Sea:
> A bended bow is lifted in heaven. . . ."

80

Head of Job. About 1825. Pencil. $10\frac{1}{4} \times 7\frac{7}{8}$ (26 × 19·8). Geoffrey Keynes, Esq., London.

A drawing apparently connected with the Illustrations of the Book of Job, *engraved by Blake and published in 1826.*

JOHN FLAXMAN
1755–1826

81 (above)

Figure studies. Pen and Indian ink wash. $3\frac{1}{8}\times6\frac{1}{8}$ (7·8 × 15·5). Inscribed "71" and "Happy Shipwreck". British Museum, 1888–5–3–70.

81 (below)

Figure studies. Pen and Indian ink wash. $3\frac{9}{16}\times5\frac{3}{4}$ (9 × 14·2). Inscribed "71". British Museum, 1888–5–3–75.

Apparently studies for illustrations (unpublished ?) to a work named The Happy Shipwreck.

THOMAS GIRTIN
1775–1802

82

Study of houses (St George's Row, Tyburn). About 1800–2. Pen and bistre wash. $4\times7\frac{7}{8}$ (10·2 × 20). British Museum, 1890–5–12–90.

83

La Rue St-Denis, Paris. 1802. Pen and Indian ink wash. $9\frac{1}{4}\times18\frac{7}{8}$ (23·5 × 48). Musée Carnavalet, Paris.

A drawing made for Girtin's etchings of Paris—for the View of the Gate of St. Denis, taken from the suburbs, *etched and published in September 1802. After Girtin's death his etchings were aquatinted and published in 1803 as* A Selection of Twenty of the most Picturesque Views in Paris and its environs. *Another version of the drawing (Sir Edmund Bacon's Collection: Girtin and Loshak,* The Art of Thomas Girtin, *1954, Plate 89) shows the street empty of traffic and figures.*

WILLIAM DANIELL
1769–1837

84

Stack at Bosherston, Pembrokeshire. 1813. Pencil, heightened with white chalk, on toned paper. $6\frac{1}{4}\times9\frac{1}{4}$ (16 × 23·5). British Museum, 1867–10–12–346.

From vol. 2 of Sketches by William Daniell R.A. in the British Museum. The sketches were made for his magnum opus, the 308 aquatints of A Voyage around Great Britain, *1814–25.*

85

Carlingford Castle. 1828. Pencil and slight watercolour. $6\frac{1}{2}\times9\frac{3}{8}$ (16·5 × 23·9). Colonel Thomas Sutton, F.S.A.

One of a series of Irish subjects which Daniell drew for a continuation of A Voyage around Great Britain *which was never carried out.*

J. M. W. TURNER
1775–1851

86

On the sands. About 1826–32. Black and white chalk on blue paper. $5\frac{1}{2}\times7\frac{1}{2}$ (14 × 19). British Museum, Turner Bequest CCLX (101).

A page from a sketchbook filled with drawings made in France, when Turner was in his fifties.

87

Study of a cutter. 1802. Black and white chalk on brown tinted paper. $17\frac{3}{8}\times10\frac{3}{4}$ (44·1 × 27·2). British Museum, Turner Bequest LXXXI (75).

One of several drawings made after a stormy landing at Calais in 1802, which suggested to Turner his painting Calais Pier: An English packet arriving, *exhibited in 1803 and now in the National Gallery.*

88

The jetty. About 1834. Black, white and red chalk on brown paper. $5\frac{1}{2}\times9$ (14 × 22·8). British Museum, Turner Bequest CCLXXXII (38a).

89

Study for Sun rising through Vapour. About 1806–7. Black and white chalk on blue paper. $17\frac{1}{8}\times10\frac{3}{4}$ (43·5 × 27·2). Inscribed "Study Calm". British Museum, Turner Bequest LXXXI (40).

Study for a painting which Turner seems to have known as Calm, *before he exhibited it in 1807 at the Royal Academy as* Sun rising through Vapour: Fishermen cleaning and selling Fish. *It is now in the National Gallery. See National Gallery Catalogues. The British School, by Martin Davies, 1946, pp. 147–8.*

90

A silent pool. About 1806–10. Sepia wash. $7\frac{1}{4} \times 10\frac{7}{8}$ (18·4×27·6). British Museum, Turner Bequest CXVI (G).

One of the sepia drawings made for the series of engravings which Turner published from 1807 to 1819 as his Liber Studiorum. *This drawing was not engraved.*

91

St Peter's, Rome. 1819. Water-colour. $16 \times 10\frac{1}{16}$ (40·7×25·5). British Museum, Turner Bequest CLXXXVII (52).

Turner visited Italy for the first time in 1819, making (especially in Rome and its neighbourhood) some of the most serene and compelling water-colour drawings of his whole lifetime. Most of them combine breadth and detail. This, and a companion drawing in the same sketchbook, record the first vision of colour and vastness and depth in a great building which was probably St Peter's (cf. the finished drawing of St Peter's reproduced, Plate V, in Turner's Water-colours at Farnley Hall, ed. A. J. Finberg, 1912.) For Turner's Rome drawings, see Ashby, Turner's Visions of Rome, *1925.*

92

The blacksmith's shop. c. 1806–7. Brown and black wash. $7\frac{5}{8} \times 10\frac{3}{4}$ (19·3 ×27·4). British Museum, Turner Bequest CXVI (H).

A drawing giving the composition, at least the disposition more or less of light and dark, of Turner's painting. The Blacksmith's Shop, *exhibited at the Academy in 1807 (now Tate Gallery, No. 478). However, the drawing (see* A silent pool *above) was made for the* Liber Studiorum, *though it was never engraved.*

JOHN CONSTABLE
1776–1837

93

Trees and water on the Stour (?) About 1829. Sepia wash over pencil, on paper with an 1829 watermark. $8\times6\frac{1}{4}$ (20·3×16·2). Victoria and Albert Museum, 250–1888.

94

Waterloo Bridge. About 1826. Pen and sepia wash and pencil. $6\frac{1}{2}\times10\frac{3}{4}$ (16·6×27·4). Victoria and Albert Museum, 604–1888.

Waterloo Bridge over the Thames was opened by the Prince Regent in 1817. Constable cherished the subject for years, exploring it in drawings, including this one, sketches in oil and large-scale versions. At last he exhibited the Opening of Waterloo Bridge *in 1832, working on the picture (now in the collection of Lord Glenconner) for two more years after the exhibition.*

95

Stoke by Nayland, Suffolk. Sepia wash over pencil. $5\times7\frac{1}{4}$ (12·8×18·4). Victoria and Albert Museum, 261–1876.

96

Banks of the canal near Newbury. 1821. Pencil and Indian ink wash. $6\frac{5}{8}\times10$ (16·9×25·5). Inscribed "Banks of the Canal near Newbury Berks, June 4 1821". Victoria and Albert Museum, 284–1888.

97

Stone in the garden, Coleorton. 1823. Pencil and Indian ink wash. $9\frac{5}{8}\times7$ (24·4×17·8). Inscribed on back "Stone in the garden, Coleorton Hall". Victoria and Albert Museum, 251–1888.

Coleorton Hall was the residence of Sir George Beaumont, amateur painter and connoisseur and friend of Wordsworth, Coleridge, Constable, etc.

98

Figure on the shore. 1835. Pencil. $4\frac{13}{16}\times7\frac{9}{16}$ (12·3 × 19·2). Victoria and Albert Museum, 316–1888 (page 3).

99

Family group. Pencil. $8\frac{9}{16}\times6\frac{3}{4}$ (21·8×17). British Museum, 1896–8–21–12.

100

Trees at Fittleworth. 1835. Pencil. $4\frac{13}{16}\times7\frac{9}{16}$ (12·2× 19·2). Inscribed in artist's hand "Fittleworth 16 July 1835". Victoria and Albert Museum, 316–1888 (page 29).

From the same sketchbook as Figure on the shore *above.*

101

Sketch at Fittleworth. 1835. Pencil. $4\frac{13}{16} \times 7\frac{9}{16}$ (12·2 × 19·2). Inscribed in artist's hand "Fittleworth July 16 1835". Victoria and Albert Museum, 316–1888.

Also from the same sketchbook as Figure on the shore *above.*

J. S. COTMAN
1782–1842

102

On the Greta. About 1805. Black chalk and wash on grey paper. 13 × 10½ (32·6 × 26·5). Tate Gallery, 3635.

103

Durham. About 1805. Black chalk and wash on grey paper. 9¼ × 10⅛ (23·6 × 25·8). Tate Gallery, 3634.

WILLIAM MULREADY
1786–1863

104

Profile on the wall: sketch for The Origin of a Painter. About 1826. Black and white chalk on brown paper. 7⅝ × 6¾ (19·3 × 17·1). Victoria and Albert Museum, E 1857–1910.

The Origin of a Painter, *was exhibited at the Royal Academy in 1826.*

JOHN LINNELL
1792–1882

105

A doorway. 1806. Charcoal and white chalk on blue paper. 6¼ × 4¾ (16 × 12). Ashmolean Museum, Oxford.

WILLIAM MULREADY
1786–1863

106

Study of sycamore keys. 1860. Pen and ink. 7½ × 9¼ (19 × 23·5). Signed and dated "W.M. 15. 9. 60". Victoria and Albert Museum, 6488.

107

A young girl. 1826. Pen and wash. 6⅛ × 4⅜ (15·5 × 11·2). Inscribed "Nov. 3. 1826". Ashmolean Museum, Oxford.

108

Study for The Barber's Shop. About 1811. Pen and wash and white body-colour. 5⅞ × 4⅞ (15 × 12·3). Victoria and Albert Museum, 6042.

Mulready exhibited The Barber's Shop, *one of his earlier genre paintings, in 1811 at the Royal Academy.*

R. P. BONINGTON
1802–28

109

A peasant in a broad hat. Black chalk. 7 × 4¾ (17·8 × 12·2). British Museum, 1896–5–11–33.

110

Studies of costume and armour. 1825. Pencil. 10¾ × 7⅛ (27·3 × 18). Inscribed in the artist's hand "guisarmier italien 1485". British Museum, 1857–2–28–157.

Studies for Bonington's small paintings of historical romance. A guisarmier was a foot soldier armed with a gisarme, a cutting and thrusting weapon on a long staff.

111

Study of bed-hangings. 1822. Pencil. 8¼ × 5½ (20·7 × 14). Inscribed "Château de la Roche Guyon Henri 4". British Museum, 1857–2–28–144.

La Roche-Guyon is on the Seine, 76 km. from Paris, in Seine-et-Oise. Famous for its tapestries, furniture, etc., the château of the Dukes of La Rochefoucald would have been a treasury of documentation for that historical side of Bonington's art so well represented in the Wallace Collection. Cf. The Bride at Prayer *(M. Maurice Gobin) and* The Letter *(Wallace Collection), repro. Shirley,* Bonington, *1940, 54 and 140.*

112

Studies of French fisherfolk. About 1824–5. Black and red chalk, heightened with white, and water-colour, on brown paper. 7⅞ × 10 3/16 (19·8 × 26). British Museum, 1901–4–17–17.

SAMUEL PALMER
1805–81

113

Barn in a valley. 1828. Pen and brush in bistre, Indian ink and gouache, over pencil. $11\frac{1}{8} \times 17\frac{5}{8}$ ($28 \cdot 2 \times 44 \cdot 8$). Ashmolean Museum, Oxford.

One of several studies made around Shoreham in 1828 for John Linnell (see biographical note).

114

The Primitive Cottage. About 1828–9. Pen and ink and wash, heightened with white body-colour. $8\frac{7}{8} \times 10\frac{7}{8}$ ($22 \cdot 5 \times 27 \cdot 6$). Inscribed on the back, in the hand of the artist's son, A. H. Palmer, "The Primitive Cottage". Victoria and Albert Museum, E 452–1953.

115

A country road leading to a church. 1830. Sepia. $7\frac{1}{4} \times 5\frac{15}{16}$ ($18 \cdot 4 \times 15 \cdot 1$). Victoria and Albert Museum, P 34–1953.

An example of the intensifying and deliberately excessive manner in which Palmer vitalized a neo-classic pastoralism with his own symbolic, yet observed vision of landscape. His naturalism and primitivism, his "Gothic" and neo-classical interests combine. Small sepia compositions of this kind are his best work.

116

At Underriver, near Sevenoaks. About 1828–9. Pen and ink with white body-colour (which has partly darkened) on a green-blue tinted paper. $6 \times 10\frac{3}{4}$ ($15 \cdot 2 \times 27 \cdot 3$). Victoria and Albert Museum, E 454–1953.

One of the drawings combining breadth and intensity with a minuteness Palmer had learnt from Mulready and Stothard. Compare Stothard's drawing (Plate 77) of the Avon at Clifton.

CHARLES KEENE
1823–91

117

Stubble field with ruins of All Saints' Church, Dunwich. 1876. Pen and brown ink. 5×7 ($12 \cdot 7 \times 17 \cdot 8$). Ashmolean Museum, Oxford.

There are related drawings and etchings of Dunwich, where Keene stayed several times with Edward Fitzgerald. He was moved by the look of Dunwich, its history and its solitude. "This is a charming, lonely place. I used to take my pipes to the beach about ten p.m. when the populace were asleep and skirl away by the sad sea waves for an hour or so. . . . I scratched on some copper plates in the cool of the evening"— Keene to Joseph Crawhall, 1876. Of a later visit in 1877 he wrote to Crawhall, "This Dunwich is a curious little place, but interesting. All along at the base of the sandy cliff (striped with layers of rolled pebbles) you come on human bones that have dropped from the shallow alluvial soil at the top. The land is sinking all along this coast, and a great city that flourished in Saxon times and was decaying at the Norman Conquest lies miles under the sea. There is one ruined church left just at the edge of the cliff . . . so secluded is this place that at any time I can strut on the hard sand and skirl away at 'Fingal's Lament' or 'The Massacre of Glencoe' (my favourite pibroch), out of earshot of a soul." (Layard, Life and Letters of Charles Samuel Keene, 2nd ed., 1892.)

118

The Ballroom Door. Indian ink wash over pencil. $4\frac{3}{4} \times 3\frac{1}{4}$ ($12 \cdot 1 \times 8 \cdot 2$). National Gallery, Edinburgh.

119

A couple in a four-poster. About 1866. Pen and black ink. $4\frac{1}{4} \times 7\frac{1}{8}$ ($10 \cdot 7 \times 17 \cdot 9$). Another version on the back. Ashmolean Museum, Oxford.

Keene designed illustrations for an edition of Mrs Caudle's Curtain Lectures by Douglas Jerrold, published in 1866. This study in the series, however, was not engraved.

120

Standing man in profile. Pencil, touched with white, on brown paper. $5\frac{3}{8} \times 2\frac{7}{16}$ ($13 \cdot 7 \times 6 \cdot 2$). Ashmolean Museum, Oxford.

121

May: British Museum closes. About 1846–50. Black and pink chalk on grey paper. $9\frac{1}{4} \times 6\frac{1}{4}$ ($23 \cdot 4 \times 16 \cdot 1$). Signed with monogram. British Museum.

An early drawing by Keene, one of a number made by himself and John Tenniel at a friend's house for a humorous Book of Beauty (described by Layard, Life and Letters of Charles Samuel Keene, 1892, and by Hudson, Charles Keene, 1947. Hudson reproduces three more of these early chalks). This drawing belonged to a series in the album illustrating the Months.

Dante Gabriel Rossetti. Charcoal. $5\frac{1}{4} \times 4\frac{5}{8}$ ($13\cdot3 \times 11\cdot7$). Ashmolean Museum, Oxford.

D. G. Rossetti (1828–82), poet and painter and original member of the Pre-Raphaelite Brotherhood. Keene's drawing suggests the Rossetti of the late sixties and the seventies, drug-ridden and suspicious, given, as his friend Watts-Dunton wrote, to "a nervous shrinking from personal contact with any save a few intimate and constantly seen friends".

FORD MADOX BROWN
1821–93

123

Study of a man painting. 1839. Pencil with touches of white, on toned paper. $11\frac{1}{8} \times 8\frac{7}{8}$ ($28\cdot2 \times 22\cdot5$). Signed and dated "F M B Antwerp 1839". Tate Gallery, 3472.

124

An infant. 1851. Black chalk and stump, heightened with white. $9\frac{1}{4} \times 6\frac{7}{8}$ ($23\cdot5 \times 17\cdot5$). Inscribed "Arthur Gabriel Madox Brown aged 10 weeks". British Museum, 1894–6–12–7.

A study for the child in the somewhat savage and peculiar picture "Take your Son, Sir" (Tate Gallery), which Brown began in 1851 and never finished.

SIR JOHN MILLAIS
1829–96

125

Study for The Deluge. About 1849–50. Pencil, pen and wash. Squared for transference. $9\frac{1}{2} \times 16\frac{3}{8}$ ($24 \times 41\cdot6$). British Museum, 1901–5–16–8.

The Deluge *remained unpainted. The text was to have been Matthew XXIV, 38–39, "For as in the days that were before the flood they were eating and drinking, marrying and giving in marriage, until the day that Noe entered into the ark, and*

knew not until the flood came, and took them all away: so shall also the coming of the Son of man be." See J. G. Millais, The Life and Letters of Sir John Everett Millais, *1899, vol. 1, pp. 95–8, 103–5.*

126

Accepted. 1853. Pen and ink. 10×7 ($25\cdot4 \times 17\cdot8$). Inscribed "Accepted John Everett Millais 1853". Private Collection.

One of a series of pen designs made when Millais found himself in love with Euphemia Ruskin, the wife of John Ruskin, whom he afterwards married. In several of them, all emotionally dramatic, it appears to be Mrs Ruskin who is depicted, in a role of innocence with a guilty or unfortunate Millais. Cf. the companion piece Rejected, *reproduced in Ironside and Gere,* Pre-Raphaelite Painters, *1948, where both are discussed, together with a quotation from J. G. Millais, that his father's aim had been to illustrate "the various tragedies of sin and temptation which assail the lot of man".*

127

The race-meeting. 1853. Pen and ink. 10×7 ($25\cdot4 \times 17\cdot8$). Signed and dated "J.E.M. 1853". Ashmolean Museum, Oxford.

According to Ironside and Gere, Pre-Raphaelite Painters, *p. 41, this drawing was a result of a visit to the racecourse at Epsom in May 1853. Among the "tragic scenes" he observed was the scene in a carriage: "a woman crying bitterly, evidently a paramour of the man who was languidly lolling back flushed with drink and trying to look unconcerned at the woman's grief. This was probably caused by a notice that his losses that day obliged him to do without her society for the future." It is another of the scenes of "sin and temptation".*

J. A. M. WHISTLER
1834–1903

128

Rosa Corder. About 1876. Pen and ink. $5\frac{13}{16} \times 3\frac{1}{2}$ ($14\cdot7 \times 8\cdot8$). British Museum, 1914–4–6–1.

A study for the celebrated Portrait of Miss Rosa Corder: Arrangement in Black and Brown, *which Whistler painted in 1876. Rosa Corder was an artist who lived with Charles Augustus Howell. The germ of drawing and painting was the sight of her relieved against the black door of Whistler's studio in Lindsay Row.*

C. A. COLLINS
1828–73

129

Study for a picture. Pen and brown ink. $9\frac{1}{2} \times 5\frac{3}{4}$ $(24 \times 14\cdot5)$. British Museum, 1891–4–4–22.

The picture would have been one of the realistic pieces of modern fiction of the Pre-Raphaelite era: the telegraph clerk in a railway office takes down a message about an accident.

J. A. M. WHISTLER
1834–1903

130

A girl reading. Black crayon on brown paper. $11 \times 7\frac{1}{8}$ $(27\cdot9 \times 18)$. Glasgow University, Birnie Philip Gift.

F. H. POTTER
1845–87

131

Study of a girl at rest. Black chalk. $9\frac{3}{8} \times 12\frac{5}{8}$ $(23\cdot8 \times 32)$. Tate Gallery, 5446.

The girl at rest in this serene drawing may be the "dearest friend", the "pretty model working in some position in a board-school", whom W. B. Yeats remembered sitting at the side of the painting throne at North End, Hampstead, "a book in her hand and my father hearing her say a Latin lesson". W. B. Yeats, Reveries over Childhood and Youth, *1915.*

G. M. HOPKINS
1844–89

132 (above)

Man lying down. Pencil. Page $4\frac{1}{2} \times 3$ $(11\cdot4 \times 7\cdot6)$. Reverend J. Meskell, S.J., and the Society of Jesus.

132 (below)

An iris. 1863. Pencil. Page $4\frac{1}{2} \times 3$ $(11\cdot4 \times 7\cdot6)$. Inscribed in the artist's hand "Manor Farm. Shanklin. July 8. 1863". Reverend J. Meskell, S.J., and the Society of Jesus.

133 (above)

On the Bollen, Cheshire. Pencil. Page $4\frac{1}{2} \times 3$ $(11\cdot4 \times 7\cdot6)$. Inscribed in the artist's hand "On the Bollen, Cheshire". Reverend J. Meskell, S.J., and the Society of Jesus.

133 (below)

Study of water. 1873. Pencil. Page $4\frac{1}{2} \times 3$ $(11\cdot4 \times 7\cdot6)$. Inscribed in the artist's hand "Balaglas, Isle of Man. Aug. 12, '73". Reverend J. Meskell, S.J., and the Society of Jesus.

W. R. SICKERT
1860–1942

134

Jack ashore. 1910. Pencil and red chalk. $13\frac{1}{2} \times 10$ $(34\cdot4 \times 25\cdot5)$. Signed "Sickert". Arts Council of Great Britain.

Another version is reproduced by Emmons, Life and Opinions of Walter Richard Sickert, *1941.*

135

Off to the pub. Pencil and pen. $10\frac{1}{2} \times 8\frac{1}{2}$ $(26\cdot8 \times 21\cdot6)$. Signed "Sickert". Arts Council of Great Britain.

136

Living marionettes. Black, white and red chalk, with pen and ink, on brown paper. $12 \times 9\frac{5}{8}$ $(30\cdot4 \times 24\cdot5)$. Signed "Sickert". Victoria and Albert Museum, E 1949–1926.

J. M. SWAN
1847–1910

137

Study of a seal. Black and white chalk on dark grey paper. $12\frac{1}{16} \times 6\frac{1}{2}$ $(30\cdot7 \times 16\cdot5)$. British Museum, 1911–1–14–12.

GWEN JOHN
1876–1939

138

Study of a baby asleep. Charcoal. $7\frac{1}{4} \times 6\frac{1}{2}$ $(18\cdot2 \times 16\cdot4)$. Stamped with facsimile signature "Gwen John". Edwin John, Esq., Paris.

139

Girl standing, with landscape. Charcoal. $11\frac{5}{8} \times 9\frac{1}{4}$ (29·5×23·4). Stamped with facsimile signature "Gwen John". Edwin John, Esq., Paris.

140

Profile of an old woman seated. Charcoal. $8\frac{3}{4} \times 6\frac{1}{2}$ (22·2×16·5). Stamped with facsimile signature "Gwen John". Edwin John, Esq., Paris.

141

Study of girl with a vacant smile. Charcoal. $9\frac{7}{8} \times 8\frac{1}{4}$ (24·9×20·9) Stamped with facsimile signature "Gwen John". Edwin John, Esq., Paris.

142

Profile of a French workman. Charcoal on grey paper. $7\frac{7}{8} \times 5\frac{7}{8}$ (19·9×14·8). Stamped with facsimile signature "Gwen John". Edwin John, Esq., Paris.

LIST OF ARTISTS